Using ISO 9001 in Healthcare

Also available from ASQ Quality Press:

Lean Doctors: A Bold and Practical Guide to Using Lean Principles to Transform Healthcare Systems, One Doctor at a Time
Aneesh Suneja with Carolyn Suneja

Quality Function Deployment and Lean Six Sigma Applications in Public Health
Grace L. Duffy, John W. Moran, and William Riley

The Public Health Quality Improvement Handbook
Ron Bialek, John W. Moran, and Grace L. Duffy

Root Cause Analysis and Improvement in the Healthcare Sector: A Step-by-Step Guide
Bjørn Andersen, Tom Fagerhaug, and Marti Beltz

Solutions to the Healthcare Quality Crisis: Cases and Examples of Lean Six Sigma in Healthcare
Soren Bisgaard, editor

On Becoming Exceptional: SSM Health Care's Journey to Baldrige and Beyond
Sister Mary Jean Ryan, FSM

Journey to Excellence: Baldrige Health Care Leaders Speak Out
Kathleen Goonan, editor

A Lean Guide to Transforming Healthcare: How to Implement Lean Principles in Hospitals, Medical Offices, Clinics, and Other Healthcare Organizations
Thomas G. Zidel

Benchmarking for Hospitals: Achieving Best-in-Class Performance without Having to Reinvent the Wheel
Victor Sower, Jo Ann Duffy, and Gerald Kohers

Lean-Six Sigma for Healthcare, Second Edition: A Senior Leader Guide to Improving Cost and Throughput
Greg Butler, Chip Caldwell, and Nancy Poston

Lean Six Sigma for the Healthcare Practice: A Pocket Guide
Roderick A. Munro

To request a complimentary catalog of ASQ Quality Press publications, call 800-248-1946, or visit our Web site at http://www.asq.org/quality-press.

Using ISO 9001 in Healthcare

Applications for Quality Systems, Performance Improvement, Clinical Integration, and Accreditation

James M. Levett, MD
Robert G. Burney, MD

ASQ Quality Press
Milwaukee, Wisconsin

American Society for Quality, Quality Press, Milwaukee, WI 53203
© 2011 by ASQ
All rights reserved. Published 2011.
Printed in the United States of America.

17   16   15   14   13   12   5   4   3   2

Library of Congress Cataloging-in-Publication Data

Levett, James M., 1949–
Using ISO 9001 in healthcare: applications for quality systems, performance improvement, clinical integration, and accreditation / James M. Levett, Robert G. Burney.
    p.; cm.
Includes bibliographical references and index.
ISBN 978-0-87389-808-9 (alk. paper)
1. Medical care—Standards. 2. Medical care—Quality control. 3. Total quality
management. I. Burney, Robert G., 1936- II. American Society for Quality. III. Title.
[DNLM: 1. Delivery of Health Care—standards. 2. Total Quality Management—
standards. W 84.1]
RA399.A1L48 2011
362.1068'4—dc22

2011012884

*NOTE: The views expressed by Dr. Burney are his personal views and do not necessarily
reflect those of the Department of State or the U. S. Government.*

Publisher: William A. Tony
Acquisitions Editor: Matt T. Meinholz
Project Editor: Paul O'Mara
Production Administrator: Randall Benson

ASQ Mission: The American Society for Quality advances individual,
organizational, and community excellence worldwide through learning, quality
improvement, and knowledge exchange.

Attention Bookstores, Wholesalers, Schools, and Corporations: ASQ Quality
Press books, video, audio, and software are available at quantity discounts with
bulk purchases for business, educational, or instructional use. For information,
please contact ASQ Quality Press at 800-248-1946, or write to ASQ Quality Press,
P.O. Box 3005, Milwaukee, WI 53201-3005.

To place orders or to request ASQ membership information, call 800-248-1946.
Visit our Web site at www.asq.org/quality-press.

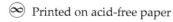 Printed on acid-free paper

Quality Press
600 N. Plankinton Ave.
Milwaukee, WI 53203-2914
E-mail: authors@asq.org

The Global Voice of Quality™

Dedication

*This book is dedicated to all healthcare providers
who strive to improve our delivery system.*

Contents

List of Figures and Tables

Foreword

Albert Einstein once said "The definition of insanity is doing the same thing over and over again and expecting different results."

In response to the healthcare crisis in the United States (spiraling costs that threaten bankruptcy, deteriorating outcomes, serious patient safety issues, and a decrease in consumer trust), politicians, academicians, payers, purchasers, and provider leaders are attempting to overhaul our faltering system and put in place cost controls and quality improvement mechanisms to right the ship for both the near and long term.

Many of these reforms are specified in recent federal legislation, including:

1. Incentives for implementation of health IT and achievement of "meaningful use" of health IT by providers;

2. Reorganization of medical practices and hospitals into "accountable care organizations" to rationalize their consumption of healthcare by putting them fiscally at risk for over-utilization, under-utilization, and mis-utilization of services;

3. Development and funding of patient safety organizations;

4. Proliferation of hundreds of "demonstration projects" to test the validity of one theory or another and/or the utility and cost-effectiveness of one change intervention or another, usually without ensuring that the vast sums expended lead to sustainability of proven concepts and/or the ability to transfer what has been learned from one organization to another.

Most of the thinking driving these innovations is led by clinicians and is, therefore, influenced heavily by the centuries old "medical model" of thinking. As such, it is usually focused on the clinical dimension of healthcare because that is what those currently in charge are most familiar with and what has generally worked for them in the past.

I believe that in some ways this approach comes close to meeting Albert Einstein's definition of insanity.

As the healthcare industry becomes less like a cottage industry and more like a corporation, the cultures and values of all healthcare stakeholders will evolve accordingly. With this type of change in healthcare delivery systems, it seems likely that those with operational, cultural, and fiscal responsibilities for the delivery of high-quality, cost-efficient, and consumer-acceptable healthcare will begin to adopt and master the techniques and quality systems that have made it possible for other industries and service organizations worldwide to make stunning advances in products, services, and organizational culture.

Such are the universal systems and tools discussed and described in great detail in this book: the general concepts of a quality management system and the ISO 9000 family of standards. Healthcare organizations of any type that are compliant with these standards are effectively deploying process improvement tools such as statistical process control, Lean, and Six Sigma while also changing their values, beliefs, and cultures to maximize their ability to provide world-class services and products in accordance with customer demand. In truth, in order to succeed in the "new-order healthcare system," each organization will have to embark on a continuous journey to improve their quality, processes, and culture. Healthcare organizations, being "complex adaptive systems," will have to adopt and utilize the systems approach to survive and flourish.[2]

Drs. Burney and Levett have provided in-depth explanations of the theory and science behind these systems while at the same time citing practical examples from their own experiences in healthcare entities of the necessary considerations, methodologies, metrics, successes, failures, and benefits attendant to the use of the ISO 9001 quality management system.

In essence they have, in this work, achieved the following goals and objectives:

1. They have made the case exquisitely for the adoption of ISO in healthcare;

2. They have skillfully acknowledged that it is a foreign concept (language) for healthcare providers;

3. They have effectively taught us by example how ISO can and is being implemented; and finally,

4. They have explained the likely detrimental consequences of not engaging in its use.

We are, indeed, indebted to these two pioneers for skillfully and understandably bringing this methodology for effective, needed, and sustainable change to healthcare.

Almost five years ago, the Institute of Medicine and National Academy of Engineering published the third in a series of IOM reports on the sad state of our healthcare system.[3] This report noted that "a real impact on quality, efficiency and sustainability of the health care system can be achieved only by using health care delivery engineering." Sadly, this report was all but ignored. I believe that Drs. Burney and Levett have made a valuable contribution in support of the IOM-NAE recommendation and that we should all join in thanking them!

Joseph A. Fortuna, MD
CEO, Prism, Michigan, USA and
Chair, ASQ Healthcare Division

References

1. James C. Robinson, *The Corporate Practice of Medicine* (California / Milbank Books on Health and the Public, 1999) ISBN: 9780520220768

2. James W. Begun, Brenda Zimmerman, and Kevin Dooley, "Health Care Organizations as Complex Adaptive Systems," in *Advances in Health Care Organization Theory*, S. M. Mick and M. Wyttenbach (eds). (San Francisco: Jossey-Bass, 2003).

3. Proctor P. Reid, W. Dale Compton, Jerome H. Grossman, and Gary Fanjiang (eds.), *Building a Better Delivery System: A New Engineering/Health Care Partnership*, Committee on Engineering and the Health Care System, National Academy of Engineering, Institute of Medicine, ISBN: 0-309-65406-8, National Academies Press at: http://www.nap.edu/catalog/11378.html

Preface

While sitting in a meeting about tools for healthcare improvement, we suddenly looked at each other with the same thought: "We should write a book!" The tools and techniques being discussed in the meeting were down in the weeds—useful for specific problems, but missing the big picture. Each of us had instituted ISO 9001 as a management system in our own healthcare settings—one a multi-specialty private practice group and the other a government primary care practice. We knew that ISO 9001 could provide the big-picture approach that healthcare needs, and this book was conceived to present that belief to a wider audience.

Healthcare professionals deal with quality issues frequently in the current era of cost containment and reform. These range from collecting data for Medicare and Medicaid (CMS) to managing accreditation and certification issues for regulatory entities. This work is time consuming and necessary, but all too often the quality programs are not sustained and are ineffective due to the lack of a system or culture to support and focus the work. We believe that a quality management system (QMS) is one solution to the problem, and this book has been written to describe the general concept of designing and implementing the ISO 9001 QMS in the healthcare setting.

The tools and techniques being discussed in our meeting were useful for specific problems but failed to address the issue of how the organization was run. Problems and solutions derived from control charts, Six Sigma, or Pareto charts were not sustained because they were not embedded in the culture of the organization. We had seen how ISO improved the efficiency of our very different organizations, and we wrote this book to explain those benefits to others.

We begin with an explanation of management systems to contrast them with other tools and techniques for process improvement. The ISO standards were originally written for the manufacturing industry, so some interpretation of the standards for healthcare seemed appropriate. Change is always difficult and is particularly so when it affects basic concepts of how the organization operates. Culture plays an important role in making institutional change. Although support at the top is important, effective change of a fundamental nature requires consideration of the organization's culture. We tell our individual stories about how we instituted ISO 9001 in our respective healthcare institutions (Chapters 8 and 9). We next present the experiences of others who have instituted ISO in hospitals and other healthcare settings. We visited and talked with CEOs and quality officers in hospitals and other healthcare organizations that had experience with ISO 9001. In every instance, we heard remarkably similar stories of initial reluctance followed eventually by enthusiastic acceptance, as employees saw the benefits of this disciplined approach to management. Remarkably, even institutions where ISO 9001 registration was not required or that had limited financial resources maintained their ISO registration because of the perceived value to their organizations.

Finally, we address the potential for using ISO management concepts in community settings such as accountable care organizations, health information exchanges, or patient safety organizations.

At the end of the day, we believe that ISO 9001 as a management system facilitates the workings of the organization. It focuses employee efforts on stated goals and provides documentation of results. Perhaps that's enough.

Acknowledgements

I would like to thank the many people who have supported me over the last 20 years as I've attempted to discover and understand quality systems in healthcare. In particular, I would like to thank my good friend Ray Carey, who taught me the basics of quality concepts and the fine points of understanding and using statistical process control charts. Ray has been an inspiration to me for many years. I am grateful for the opportunity I had at Lutheran General Hospital in Park Ridge, Illinois, during my tenure there to meet interesting and knowledgeable providers focused on quality and improving the patient care experience. My colleagues in the Healthcare Division of the American Society for Quality deserve special mention for their support and friendship, most importantly Mickey Christensen, Douglas Dotan, Joe Fortuna, and Ray Zielke. Travis Mathison did an outstanding job of proofreading the manuscript and I am indebted to him for his efforts.

I am also grateful to the physicians, nurses, administrators, mid-level providers, and other staff at Physicians' Clinic of Iowa for the support they have given me over the last ten years as we came to understand and develop a quality management system within our organization. Special thanks to Joan Atkinson, who has devoted a great deal of time and energy to helping establish and maintain our quality system at PCI.

Most importantly, I would like to express my sincere appreciation to my wife Paula and my children, who over the years have been very understanding about the time I have spent on various quality projects. They have suffered through many discussions about quality, Lean–Six Sigma, ISO 9001, and the like.

– James M. Levett, MD

I would like to thank my uncle, Kenneth Hewins, for sharing the journalism genes that compelled me to write and my professors at DePauw University who taught me how.

– Robert G. Burney, MD

DNV Healthcare uses ISO 9001 in its hospital accreditation process and Yehuda Dror, President of DNV Healthcare, Inc., made important contributions to Chapter 10 and provided contacts with hospitals that had been accredited by DNV. We contacted several of these institutions and are particularly grateful for the time given by Deb McKee, RN, and Sonnie Bernardi, RN, of Township Memorial Hospital in St. Claire, Ohio; Claire Lee, RN, of Ball Memorial Hospital in Muncie, Indiana; and Beryl Vallejo, PhD, RN, of St. Luke's Episcopal Health System in Houston, Texas.

We also appreciate the contacts provided by Steve Pettyjohn for rehabilitation facilities in Indiana. Among several who shared their experiences were Debra Seman and Vickie Carter-Stanford from ARC Opportunities in Howe, Indiana, and Steve Hinkle of Easter Seals ARC in Fort Wayne, Indiana.

No work such as this happens in a vacuum. We owe much to our editors at ASQ for encouraging us and providing valuable feedback for completion of the manuscript. Finally, we are extremely grateful to all who shared their time and experiences with us.

— The Authors

Introduction

These are interesting times in healthcare. About the only certainty is that things will be different next year. Factors driving change include reduced reimbursements, ever-changing regulations, nursing shortages, compliance requirements that change constantly, and competition for patients from an increasing variety of providers and institutions. There is great concern over the amount of money the United States spends on healthcare, both in absolute terms and as a percent of our GDP. Most of the proposed solutions involve reducing the amount of healthcare provided, but there are also thoughts about bundling services to obtain package pricing. Suggestions for price competition, as seen in other industries, have been voted down by Congress, but that option may return. All of these are threats to the status quo for healthcare providers, whether physician offices or multi-hospital systems. Dealing with these challenges requires an effective management system.

Each of the authors has instituted ISO 9001:2008 as a management system: one in a multi-specialty group practice, the other in a global government healthcare system. Our reasons were different, but in both cases, we established a management system that could respond to our diverse needs without adding expenses to our institutions.

ISO has a scant presence in healthcare, partly because the standards were originally written for the manufacturing industry and retain much of that language. This makes it difficult to understand for many in healthcare. In this book, we outline our personal experiences and explain some aspects of the ISO standards as they apply to the healthcare industry. We also explore the adoption of ISO as a management system in other healthcare settings and explore its usefulness in proposed scenarios in the current discussions about healthcare.

We believe that ISO offers an orderly, disciplined approach to managing a healthcare organization. As with any system, it can be done poorly and will then not bring the anticipated benefits. However, when applied conscientiously, the ISO management system will provide a framework for improvement efforts and the discipline to demonstrate what must be improved.

Healthcare professionals, like all employees, want to work in a progressive environment and will seek organizations that have adopted a fresh approach to healthcare delivery. Everyone wants to play on the first team.

Healthcare must be changed. We have grown complacent and have failed to improve our delivery system in the 12 years since the Institute of Medicine published *To Err is Human.* It is time now to implement a new paradigm of quality management that will bring about clear, concise, and measurable improvements, reduce errors, and enable positive change in healthcare delivery systems.

1

Quality Management Systems in Healthcare: What Are They and Why Are They Useful?

The concept of a quality management system (QMS) was introduced into U.S. industry more than 20 years ago. Although various organizations and businesses have developed and refined the concepts of quality management over the years, many of the principles remain unchanged. For example, in the late 1980s, the big three automakers were concerned that they were dependent upon thousands of suppliers, with no way of determining which suppliers provided quality products. The automobile industry responded by adopting a series of standards called QS 9000. ISO standards will be discussed in Chapter 2, but suffice it to say that the ISO standards were established to support quality and standardization in international commerce. Suppliers were required to become QS 9000 certified if they were to continue doing business with the three big automakers. Some companies, such as Ford Motor Company, have developed quality management systems within their organizations. In 1987 the Malcolm Baldrige National Quality Award was instituted to help improve quality and productivity by establishing guidelines and criteria that can be used by businesses, governmental organizations, and non-profit organizations in the process of evaluating their own quality improvement efforts. The Baldrige criteria for performance excellence have been used throughout service and manufacturing industries as well as in governmental, healthcare, and educational realms and have become increasingly recognized as a worthwhile goal for companies to pursue. The idea of a QMS is thus simple in concept but complex in practice as various types of systems have been developed.

Through analyzing these quality management systems, we see a number of principles emerge that are useful to review. Common features of Baldrige and ISO quality management systems include: leadership, strategic planning, customer and market focus, information management, agility, continual improvement, innovation, document management, human resources management, process management, and business results. Other types of quality methods have also been developed, most importantly Lean and Six Sigma. In some instances, these methods serve as quality management systems when they are imbedded into the culture of the organization and impact all aspects of the organization. When this is not the case, however, they function as tools rather than quality management systems.

THE PROCESS APPROACH

A process approach is used in most quality management systems. This essentially means that work is defined as a process, with inputs to the process resulting in outputs that then serve as inputs to another process (Figure 1.1). Categories of processes include products, services, resources, and information. As work is broken down into process steps, process diagrams and flow charts can be utilized to better understand the overall work mechanism and see relationships. The next important principle is that processes are linked together to form systems, as outputs of one process become inputs to another. Systems theory includes several ideas worth noting. The first is that a system cannot be optimized if one part of it becomes more important/efficient than other parts. Thus, all parts of a system must be equally important/improved to truly optimize the entire system. Work in healthcare is very much a system that must be understood and, as in other systems, it must be carefully managed. In the early process approach, an organization deals with problems on a reactionary basis. As systems thinking is adopted, strategic and operational goals are better understood and coordination begins. Aligned and integrated approaches are a more mature level of process management, and in these cases the processes are regularly evaluated and repeatable. Efficiencies are thus gained across the organization as the process approach is utilized and improvements are made.

Process Management Excellence

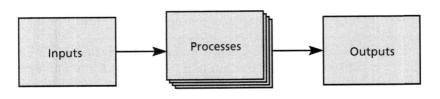

Figure 1.1 The process approach.

It is important to understand that the process approach is really a management strategy. Using a process approach, managers and leaders can manage processes, the interaction between processes, and the inputs and outputs that link processes to each other.

BUILDING THE SYSTEM

Once a process approach is in place, it must be refined to build a system. In most quality management systems, quality planning is introduced with the initial task of clearly defining the mission, vision, and values of the organization. That is, why the organization exists, what it wants to become, and what is important to it. The QMS then identifies key strategic goals and objectives (Figure 1.2). Requirements for these goals and objectives can be determined and benchmarks may also be identified. The next step is to define key processes within the organization. Most organizations will have five to ten key processes that encompass most of its work. In healthcare, these processes may include everything from registration and scheduling to clinical care delivery and measuring performance and outcomes (Figure 1.3).

For each process, it is important to define the requirements for both inputs and outputs. In order to monitor goals and objectives, measurements are chosen that are related to both processes and outcomes. An example would be monitoring the appropriate administration of antibiotics during and after a surgical procedure (the process) and then tracking the incidence of wound infections in the post-operative period (the outcome).

Thus, when building a QMS, one can set quality goals and objectives that are measured and controlled in a way that results in improvement over time.

Define:

Mission

Vision

Values

Strategic Goals/Objectives

Figure 1.2 Mission, vision, values, strategy.

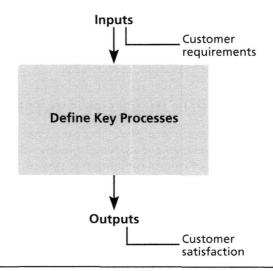

Figure 1.3 Defining the key processes.

MANAGING THE KEY PROCESSES

After defining the key processes, our next step is to manage them. Within the context of a QMS, several features may be used. These include a controlled document system, auditing, corrective and preventive action plans, measurement and data collection, and management review to oversee the system (Figure 1.4). These features comprise the core components of a QMS.

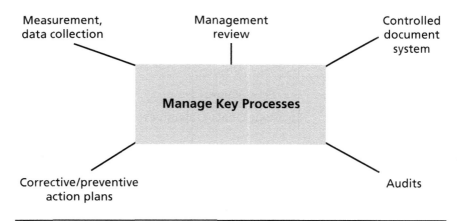

Figure 1.4 Managing the key processes.

IMPROVING THE KEY PROCESSES

The next step is improving the key processes. Many different tools are available for this purpose and they can generally be easily incorporated into a QMS. Tools include design and redesign, risk assessment, Six Sigma, Lean, statistical process control, PDCA, strategic planning, a balanced scorecard, and many others (Figure 1.5).

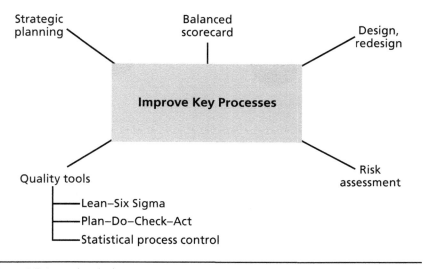

Figure 1.5 Improving the key processes.

One important tool common to quality systems is the Plan–Do–Check–Act or PDCA cycle (Figure 1.6). This methodology, originally described by W. Edwards Deming, can be used to manage and improve any process. The steps are as follows:

Plan

Identify the objectives and define the processes necessary to deliver results and the expected output. Focus on the output, since it will assist in designing the appropriate specifications to help achieve the desired improvement.

Do

Implement the new processes.

Check

Develop measures for the new processes and determine whether the results were those that were expected.

Act

Analyze any differences between observed and expected results and determine which of the PDCA steps were involved. Assess where changes could be implemented to make improvement. Refine the scope as needed, keeping in mind that incremental steps are usually the most likely to succeed.

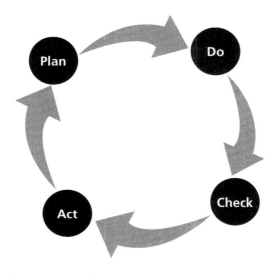

Figure 1.6 The PDCA cycle.[1]

PUTTING IT TOGETHER: THE QUALITY MANAGEMENT SYSTEM

A quality management system comprises the components described in Figure 1.6. Its goal is to address all functions that are necessary to meet all customer requirements. Its system is based on defining, managing, and improving the key processes of an organization. It is designed as a framework that will accommodate additional tools and requirements as they arise. A QMS can thus be defined as the framework or infrastructure used by an organization to support and manage its policies, procedures, practices, and planning activities. The QMS enables an organization to better meet customer expectations and decrease problems and errors.

In general, all quality management systems share several characteristics:

1. **Comprehensive.** A QMS must encompass all aspects of running the organization, from producing the goods to managing money.

2. **Scalable.** If you're running a lemonade stand, your management system can be written on the back of an envelope. However, as soon as you have enough employees that you can't get them all into the same room easily, you need a system to run things. At a very high level, management systems should adapt to companies of all sizes. Obviously, the documentation and details will vary, but the basic principles should be the same.

3. **Flexible.** Companies differ. The philosophies of chief executive officers and healthcare leaders will differ. Each organization operates in a unique environment, with differing threats and opportunities. The QMS should allow for these variations while still adhering to basic principles. A QMS such as ISO 9001 has core components (as discussed in Chapter 2), but allows for additional features to be added based on an organization's needs.

4. **Understandable.** The CEO must sell employees on his choice of a QMS, and the employees must implement the QMS every day in their work. This means it must be easily understood by workers at all educational levels.

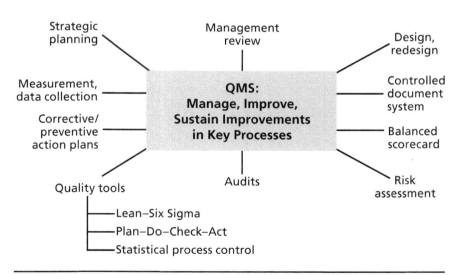

Figure 1.7 The quality management system.

THE VALUE OF A QUALITY MANAGEMENT SYSTEM

A QMS is built using a process approach to define key processes, monitor and manage them, and make sustainable improvements in a timely fashion. The framework of a QMS allows an organization to incorporate additional features as needed. For example, regulatory HIPAA requirements might be added to the system. In the QMS illustrated in Figure 1.7, the requirements would be documented in a controlled document system; audited, monitored and measured on a balanced scorecard; and managed with corrective and preventive action plans in an appropriate manner. Quality tools would be utilized when necessary and the entire system would be overseen by a management review process on a regular basis.

ADDITIONAL FEATURES OF A QMS

Many organizations today have moved toward development of a balanced scorecard, first described by Kaplan and Norton in 1992.[2] The balanced scorecard is a systematic method of aligning the strategic goals and objectives of an organization and monitoring performance. With a balanced scorecard, goals, objectives, requirements, performance measurements, and benchmarks can be monitored on a regular basis in order for managers and employees throughout the organization to understand the organization's performance. The process approach allows an organization to determine and monitor its most important processes, and then improve and control them using the balanced scorecard. It is important to have metrics that are understandable, but also to not have too many metrics.

References

1. The PDCA Cycle. With permission from creator Karn G. Bulsuk (http://blog.bulsuk.com)

2. R. Kaplan and D. Norton, "The Balanced Scorecard—Measures that Drive Performance," *Harvard Business Review* (January/February 1992): 92–100.

2

Background and Introduction to the ISO Family of Standards

The International Organization for Standardization (ISO) was founded in Geneva in 1947.[1] The original purpose of the organization was to provide standardization of technical specifications for products traded in the international marketplace. The term *ISO* is derived from the Greek *isos*, meaning equal. The choice of ISO is thus meant to suggest a standardization or "standard." More than 150 countries are members of ISO, and more than 18,000 ISO standards are used worldwide. These standards determine how various products and services are produced, and include standards for film speed, thickness of credit cards, compact disc format, screw thread number, and more. Standardization has thus served an important role in promoting quality and compatibility of products on a global basis.[2] ISO technical committees comprising representatives from interested member countries address specific standards and perform the overall work of standardization.

Over the years the concept of standardization has evolved from that of technical specifications to a broader concept of generic QMS standards. The concept was first brought to the United States by the automobile industry in the late 1980s to qualify the thousands of suppliers used by automobile manufacturers. This effort was a concrete example of competitors working together to develop a quality framework that would serve both themselves and their customers. The automobile industry described the specific standards for its suppliers in the QS 9000 system, and other industries have done the same with customized QMS standards for the particular industry.

The ISO 9001 family of QMS standards was first developed in 1987 and revised in 1994, 2000, and 2008.[3] In 2001 the American Society for Quality, in partnership with the Automotive Industry Action Group (AIAG), published a set of preliminary standards for healthcare known as the IWA-1 healthcare document.[4] At Physicians' Clinic of Iowa (PCI), this document was helpful in learning about ISO and its application in healthcare organizations; it can be obtained through the website:

www.iso.org. Since ISO rules call for a six-year limit on IWA documents, in late 2006 AIAG elected to prepare a "hybrid" replacement document based on both ISO 9001 and the Malcolm Baldrige Health Care Criteria for Performance Excellence. This new document also incorporated industry best practices applicable to the healthcare sector. The new document, entitled *Business Operating Systems (BOS) for Health Care Organizations—Requirements for Process Improvements to Achieve Excellence,* offers practical guidance to organizations of all maturity levels and can be obtained from AIAG at www.aiag.org, item number HF-2.

There are many reasons for a healthcare facility to obtain ISO certification. Establishing an ISO 9001 QMS provides for work performance consistency, stresses the process approach, defines goals and objectives for quality, provides benchmarks to measure improvements, and requires identification and evaluation of causes of poor performance. Quality management requires customer focus and continual improvement. It provides accountability within the system and ensures that the most important functions are carried out. It establishes a clear document system throughout the organization, a common language across the organization, and common identifiers for customers/patients.[5] As we will see, an organization seeking ISO registration is required to describe and implement a QMS according to the requirements of the American National Standard for quality management systems.[6] This involves writing a quality policy, quality manual, and quality objectives and then utilizing the process approach to address the other requirements of the standard.

ISO 9000 is the family of standards; an entity is registered to ISO 9001:2008. ISO 9001 requirements are based on the following eight quality management principles:

- Customer focus
- Leadership
- Involvement of people
- Process approach
- Systems approach to management
- Continual improvement
- Factual approach to decision making
- Mutually beneficial supplier relationships

The principles are imbedded within the eight clauses of ISO 9001:2008 that comprise the quality manual for an organization, and together they describe the QMS. A QMS may thus be described as a set of processes that provide direction and control of an organization's quality. Quality is defined as the degree to which a set of inherent characteristics or features fulfills the needs of patients and other customers.

The main principle is consistency. It's impossible to improve a process if everyone does it differently and the results are random. Good healthcare should not be an accident. Good results should be expected every time, and you don't get that result without planning.

In a conversation about the advantages of ISO registration for all Cunard line health units, a medical officer on the Queen Mary 2 cited his ability to serve on any ship in the fleet and know that the procedures were the same and that the nursing staff used the same protocols and forms everywhere.

The American National Standards Institute (ANSI) of the Department of Commerce represents U.S. interests in the standards writing process in Geneva. Copies of the standards are available from ISO or from the American Society for Quality (www.asq.org) in the United States for about $100.

The International Organization for Standardization in Geneva writes and publishes the standards. They do not audit organizations, and they do not provide consultations regarding their standards. Furthermore, they do not certify compliance with the standards. A registrar, which is a company authorized by ISO, will audit your organization and then issue a certificate indicating compliance with the standards.

OVERVIEW

Think of these standards as your conscience—the discipline that forces you to do what you already know you should be doing. There is nothing mysterious or onerous about this quality management system. For example, without control of documents (a required procedure), there is some level of chaos, and someone will inevitably use an obsolete form or procedure. When we started our ISO journey at the State Department, there were four slightly different procedures for obtaining a DEA registration—stored in four different places on our network. Today there is one, and everyone knows exactly where to find it.

The other significant characteristic of ISO is its plasticity or flexibility. The standards are written at a very high level, and specification of most details is left to the organization. For example, standard 4.2.3 (Control of Documents) states that documents must be approved and revised, as necessary, and must be available at points of use. However, there are no details specified regarding how the organization should accomplish those goals, and no time is specified for revision of documents—only "as necessary."

The ISO 9001 standards are brief. My paper copy is only 14 pages. By contrast, my copy of The Joint Commission standards for ambulatory care runs 208 pages, and their hospital standards occupy several volumes. In fairness, any institution that wants to be paid for providing healthcare services must also satisfy the CMS *Conditions of Participation* in addition to the ISO 9001 standards, but the combination of ISO 9001 and the CMS *Conditions of Participation* can be written in under 200 pages. The point is not so much the length of the requirements as the level of detail included. With the less prescriptive ISO 9001 approach, much more is left to the discretion of the individual healthcare facility.

Remember, these ISO standards were not written specifically for healthcare. The same standards can be used by any organization in any industry. This universal applicability also brings a challenge: healthcare workers must open their minds to recognize generic terminology. "Product realization" is not a term one finds frequently in healthcare, but there is a whole section (Section 7) in the standards about this. The challenge is to recognize that product realization just means making it happen—transforming resources into healthcare services. The Baldrige Award wrote entirely separate criteria for service industries, for manufacturing, for education, and for healthcare in order to enhance understanding within diverse industries. There was some objection at the time from those who insisted healthcare was a service industry and should use the service standards. ISO made the decision to use one set of standards for everyone—manufacturing, service, healthcare, and every other industry. There are advantages to each approach, but the ISO approach does require a bit of interpretation from time to time.

The word *quality* is used extensively in the standards and in healthcare literature, so much so that it has almost become a slang term. It is possible to go through the ISO standards and remove the word *quality* without altering the meaning of the text. Is there any real difference between a "quality management system" and a "management system?" The point here is that if the word *quality* causes problems for you, drop it. Many organizations have dropped parts of their name or decided to use only initials when the name was no longer relevant. If you go to www.asq.org, you will not find what those initials (used to) stand for. Similarly, if you visit www.jointcommission.org, you won't find JCAHO or any reference to what those initials used to mean.

PRINCIPLES FOR HEALTHCARE

From a very high level, five key tenets of ISO 9001 are particularly important for healthcare. Other aspects cannot be ignored, but these five are especially important for the healthcare industry.

Customer Focus

Some in healthcare resist using the term *customers* and admit only to having patients. Dismiss this semantic quibbling by saying, "If you don't have customers, we'll just close your office, and no one will ever know."

This is another point for translation and an open mind. Patients are, of course, customers, but they are not the only customers in healthcare. There are diverse other "interested parties" who also qualify as customers. The ISO 9001 standards require a focus on customers, all customers, and their satisfaction with the goods and services you produce. The standards require the organization to be in touch with customer needs and to document how well it is meeting them. The customer requests a service, which you provide. Then he gives feedback, which you use to modify your process for the next customer. Unfortunately, life is not that simple. As noted, there are multiple tiers of customers, including many within the same transaction or encounter. There is, of course, the patient, but there are also the patient's family and the insurance company. In most healthcare situations, physicians are also customers and probably regard the patient as one of their customers. Don't forget internal customers—employees within the institution and the investors who own it. In this complex environment, all of these customers must be considered—even when their goals are competing or incompatible. Once you convince yourself that you sincerely care about what your customers say, listening to their voices becomes much easier.

Measure, Analyze, and Improve

Healthcare settings are full of metrics. We measure patients and things that come from patients, but we seldom measure our own actions in providing care to patients. ISO requires two sorts of measures: process measures (how is it going?) and outcome measures (did it turn out well?). When a given process is not producing the desired results, it is appropriate to look at the process for reasons. The first question will be, "Was the process performed according to the written guidelines?" It is possible for a properly functioning process to produce less than desirable results, but more commonly, the written procedure was not being followed. In determining what to measure, consider time in the absence of a more obvious choice. Time is easy to understand, easy to measure, and understood by spreadsheets such as Excel. This means you can record times into a spreadsheet and know instantly how long it took from request to output. Time will not tell you exactly what is wrong, but it can indicate the step in your process where the delay occurs. When we had a concern about the length of time required to hire new nurse practitioners, a look at the time stamps in our process disclosed that our HR department was spending a month on average obtaining required information from the applicants. That's an average of one month, with a very large standard deviation. We reduced this to zero by shifting to an on-line application process in which the application cannot be submitted until all the information is included.

Process Approach

A hierarchy of terms ranges from *process* to *procedure* to *activity*, but the terminology is not as important as the higher-level concept. In thinking about key processes for your organization, ignore details but include everyone who participates. Look at this as an exercise in product line management. In a surgery center, for example, there may be a single key process—"We provide surgical services for outpatient procedures." Under this umbrella, however, there are probably four or five disciplines that contribute to the process for any given patient: registration, pre-op, operating room, and recovery. With the process approach described in Chapter 1, each of these areas would have its own written policies and procedures for how do things, but they would also participate in looking at the broad picture and how they interact. For example, when the patient arrives late and the OR is waiting, this may be the time for the registration clerk to grab her clipboard and collect information while the patient is changing clothes. When a husband leaves his office number with the registration clerk, how does that number get to the recovery nurse who will actually make the call? A hospital probably has several key processes that may interact or use the same resources at times. This makes it especially important that everyone understands the role of each process and how it works. For example, when a woman about to deliver enters the ER, you don't want the clerk to tell her to take a seat in the waiting room. Sometimes downstream participants have suggestions for other areas to facilitate the entire process. Data should be collected only once and then shared. Remember the scene in the movie *The Doctor* where the surgeon, now a patient, asks in frustration, "Don't you guys ever talk to each other?"

Document Control

True, this is only one of the six required procedures, but this one resonates so strongly with employees that it deserves special emphasis. When our employees were surveyed about positive aspects of our ISO effort, "I can find things now" was the most frequent comment. In one hospital that went from Joint Commission to DNV Healthcare accreditation, most employees cited document control as an important positive aspect of the change. In one ISO-registered engineering company, every printed document comes with a watermark that says, "Obsolete." Only the electronic copy is current. But old habits die hard, and document control will not be easy. There is a "squirrel factor" that drives us to save personal copies, either paper or electronic. Internal auditors may correct some of this, but it is also a cultural thing; change will take time. The risk, of course, is that the original may have been revised by the time you drag out your ancestral copy. The other problem area under this heading is "documents of external origin." The ideal plan is to use links to documents on outside web sites, rather than downloading a pdf copy of your very own. The CDC revises its immunization schedule at irregular intervals, so any physical or electronic copy is at risk. For all of the above reasons, the biggest change in your organization will come under the heading of document control. Take the time to do it well.

Reporting and Auditing

Hospitals have a somewhat easier time with the auditing aspect because of their tradition of auditing by The Joint Commission. It's really not the same, however. With ISO, the auditors will want to see evidence that you are in compliance with your own procedures that you wrote, rather than looking for compliance with an external standard. An ISO audit focuses first on the management system. Does the organization have a system in place for monitoring and improving key processes? Does management review occur? In order for management review to function, there must be reporting from key processes to provide data for management to act on. The very fact of collecting such data will send a message to employees that "this is what management thinks is important." In fact, this may evolve to a conversation between senior management and the process owners about how their process fits in the broad objectives of the organization.

INDIVIDUAL STANDARDS

In the following discussion, we will look at each section of the ISO 9001 standards and examine its impact for healthcare organizations, large and small. The first three sections or headings of the ISO 9001 standard require little or no action from the organization.

Section 1 asks you to define the scope of your QMS. Here, it's wise to be inclusive. Anything should be included if it has your name on the door or if it would be recognized by the public as belonging to you. The medical staff office that does credentialing should be included, but physicians themselves may be excluded if they are separate legal entities and not employees. Trying to carve out sections will create problems later in developing metrics for processes that interact with those sections. There are support services that the patient generally doesn't see, but that are nonetheless vitally important to the function of the enterprise. (For example: HR, engineering, and the guy who empties the waste basket.) In many cases, these services are not noticed when they work well. Nobody notices the air conditioning unless it's too cold where people change clothes. These should all be included in the QMS, perhaps in a separate category of "support services" in contrast to the more public key processes. The main reason to include them in the QMS is to include them in management review.

Section 2 references a dictionary of ISO terms and requires no action. It's a good idea to make this dictionary available to employees, but no specific action is required.

Section 3 defines some terms used in the rest of the standards and requires no action. Here also is the statement that the word *product* can also mean *service*.

Section 4 is where the work begins. This section contains requirements for the quality manual, control of documents, and control of records.

The organization must write a quality manual describing the quality management system. There is a tendency in healthcare to overwrite the manual. Requirements for the quality manual are fairly specific in the standards, and this can be accomplished in pages that number no more than a single digit. One strategy to minimize writing is to include, by reference, the current version of the ISO standards. This means that if the standards require something, we will do it. No need to say more. Note that the six required procedures need not be included in the manual itself—only a reference to them. In fact, it is better not to include more than necessary within the manual, so that these elements can be revised independently as separate documents.

The standards do require a statement in the manual regarding the scope of the QMS, what is included. As noted above, it's wise to be inclusive here to avoid future difficulties with the interface between what is and what is not included.

On the subject of inclusion, note that it is permissible to exclude the design and development standards (7.3) if you don't do design and development work. But someday, you might. You may decide to offer a new service or write some new software or otherwise begin doing something you haven't done before. The standards under 7.3 help ensure that it is done right. The standards are not mysterious or onerous, and you may want to resist the temptation to exclude these standards from your scope.

Another requirement for the manual is the inclusion of procedures "or reference to them." As noted above, it is probably a good idea to keep procedures out of the manual itself and just reference to them. This way, individual procedures can be revised as needed without revising everything in the manual at the same time.

The requirement for a description of the interaction between individual processes promotes process thinking within the organization. Think of it as an opportunity to do product line management. The average healthcare facility will probably offer several processes to patients, although many will use common services such as parking, registration, waiting rooms, and so on. Looking at each process individually may bring forth opportunities to eliminate waste or duplication.

Control of documents is another essential component of Section 4. Any organization will have a large number of documents—procedures and forms, for example. ISO requires that they be legible and available at the point of use. They need not be part of the quality manual or even kept in the same location. The only requirement is that those who need them can find them and use them. Many organizations use electronic documents stored on a common server. It should go without saying that this server must be backed up at defined intervals and that back-up copies should be stored in a different location. (Another precaution is to ensure that the back-up medium actually contains the files—that it is not blank.)

One problem with paper documents is that people copy them and may use the copies long after the originals have been revised. That's what document control is all about—ensuring that the current version, and only the current version, is available at the point of use.

Sometimes questions come up regarding whether a particular document must be controlled. The standards say any document that is "needed" must be controlled. This means there must be an indication of the revision status, approval for use, and the reasons for any revisions. It is useful, although not required, to give each document a number. We assigned a set of numbers between 0 and 9,999 to each section. Documents numbered 0001 thru 0099 belong to the director's office. Decimals are allowed, and many sections use decimals to indicate related documents. For example, document 2089.0 is a process that requires completion of record number 2089.1. The work instructions for this process are in document 2089.2.

An equally important question has to do with which documents need *not* be controlled. If you start with the premise that any document needed for the provision of services must be controlled, then the corollary is that if it's not needed, it need not be controlled. Examples of documents that need not be controlled include:

- A notice of the date of your Christmas party
- Your monthly newsletter
- The cafeteria menu for next week
- A request for volunteers to serve as internal auditors
- Date and location of the next management review

Note, however, that many documents the customer/patient never sees must be controlled. Procedures and records related to the billing process come to mind. The schedule for the operating room and the procedure for cleaning instruments are other examples.

A word about outside documents or "documents of external origin": We all do this, download a pdf file and reference it in our procedures. If you use this to provide services for patients, then the document must be controlled. Furthermore, since you do not have control over the revision status, someone must monitor the source to be certain you always have the current version. One easy solution is to imbed the link to the source of this document. If the document always has the same name, the link will work. Otherwise, link to the web page and invite the user to select the relevant document. Each section that uses outside documents must identify these and document that it is using the latest version.

Some outside documents are not available on the internet. Manuals for equipment come in hard copy and are not revised. Textbooks or other reference material may be published at long intervals, and older versions may be preferable at times. The only requirement is that users have the version they need and that you know what version they are using.

Control of records is as important as control of documents. Records begin life as documents but, once completed, they become records and are treated in accordance with the Control of Records policy. If you apply for a job with us, you fill out an application form, document number 1051. Once complete, this application is a record and is filed alphabetically by your last name. From this, you can see that documents can be changed, either by revision or by conversion to a record. In principle, records cannot be changed. They are generally an indication of some activity. For example, we have a document for use by our internal auditors. Once completed, it becomes a record containing the results of their audit activity. The minutes of our management review meetings are records of that activity.

Section 5 defines management responsibility. Senior management is always responsible for making sure the right things happen. It is management's job to demonstrate commitment to employees through the quality policy (QP) and the quality objectives. Part of this commitment is to appoint the management representative from within the senior management team. This person serves as a first sergeant or chief operating officer for the quality management system.

There are only three requirements for the content of the quality policy:

1. Comply with requirements (ISO standards and others)

2. Continually improve

3. Establish objectives

The QP is similar in some respects to a mission statement but has more specific requirements. A QP may thus suffice for a mission statement, but the reverse is not necessarily true. The QP should be fairly short, if it is to be understood and remembered conceptually by all employees. It's OK to have both a QP and a mission statement.

Objectives must be measurable and relevant to the organization. There is a tendency to wax eloquent here, with statements such as "improve the health of the community." In fact, most healthcare organizations have very little to do with community health. They provide healthcare services to individuals within and outside their community, and then only at the request of a physician. You will be expected to demonstrate improvement in your objectives, and this improvement should result from your activities. Be careful when stating objectives to make them relevant and quantifiable. Many healthcare organizations do contribute to their communities in diverse ways, but this is done as a civic responsibility, not part of their mission.

Section 6 addresses resource management, the management of facilities, equipment, tools, and people. In general, these are things that healthcare organizations have been doing for a long time, so Section 6 should pose no challenge. However, consistency is required within the organization: if you decide that scales must be calibrated annually, then *all* scales must be calibrated annually.

Expect to do some training of employees in ISO principles. Organizations with a history of Joint Commission audits will have an easier time, because the principle of outside standards is established. The more training you do, the easier the preparation. Internal auditors will require training in auditing beyond knowledge of the standards. The State Department found it advisable to train individuals at all levels of the organization chart. We had no tradition for outside auditing, and few employees had ever worked in a hospital. Whatever approach you take, communication is vital.

Section 7 has to do with product realization. This title is decipherable, but it takes a little effort for the English speaking healthcare audience. Once you get your arms around it, however, it is quite useful, because it includes everything necessary to make things happen.

Much of this standard relates to communication with customers, and this goes both ways. Patients need to know what you can do for them and what the steps are once they walk in the front door. You need to know what they want and what they think about your services. The first step is to convince yourself that you sincerely care about what your patients think. After that, it's easy. We once did a survey that asked whether patients had difficulty finding our office and almost 80% responded "yes." When we took this to senior management, the reply was, "We have signs. What's the matter with these patients that they can't read our signs?"

Section 8 has to do with measurement, analysis, and improvement. The first part of this standard essentially instructs the organization to do what is necessary to continually improve. Knowing that there is a problem or a potential problem is, of course, the first step. We have advocated time as a useful process metric, even when no one cares about time. Time is easy and cheap to measure. Excel does time arithmetic, so logging the date/time of the request and the date/time the service was provided can produce a scatter plot with a point for every customer. Most of the points will cluster along a single line, but sometimes there will be outliers indicating that the process took much longer. That may not be a problem, and being aware of the longer time isn't the same as knowing what the problem was. However, something about the process did not go along as usual in this case. Analysis of outliers may help prevent future problems by indicating unexpected problems. A key employee may have been on vacation, for example. That's OK if she's gone for a day or two, but other plans are indicated when the vacation goes on for several weeks.

CUSTOMER FOCUS

When considering customer satisfaction, most people instinctively turn to surveys. These are useful but shouldn't be the only means of hearing the voice of the customer. I once glanced into our recovery room and went immediately to the bedside of a patient across the room.

"Are you having pain?" I asked.

"Yes," she replied. "But how did you know?"

It was my job to know, to be aware. She was my customer, and I knew without a survey that she was having pain and that this was not a good thing. A quick IV narcotic resulted in a satisfied customer.

Similarly, it is not hard for a nurse to recognize a patient who is cold or a child who needs his mommy. Common needs may require training to promote recognition or importance, but the response should then be instinctive.

These are the "moments of truth" that Jan Carlzon wrote about, when customers interact with employees and decide what kind of company you are.[7] The trick for management is to have a system for capturing these moments collectively and analyzing them systematically in order to uncover opportunities to improve your service.

Think also about non-customers. We do paper surveys after our quarterly risk management meetings and proudly displayed the excellent approvals to our internal auditor. Then the auditor asked, "Do you ever survey those who don't come?" We typically run about 30% attendance of those who are eligible to come, but had never thought to ask the others why they stayed away.

In the surgery center, we had a formal program to interview every new employee at the end of the first month and ask, "What did your previous employer do that we should be doing?" Without this formal mechanism, that valuable information would be lost.

There was a sentence at the bottom of our paper survey that read: "Every survey is read by every employee and every manager." Once a month, the managers met to go over every customer survey and look for opportunities to address any problems reported. After that, the surveys were put out in the employee lunchroom for employees to read, which they did. This had the result of reinforcing desirable behaviors. When a patient wrote, "I was grateful when Judy brought me a warm blanket before I had to ask," everyone who read that became more cognizant of the patient's need for a warm blanket on return from the operating room.

Paper surveys should be short—one page, maximum. The first few questions should be consistent and relate to issues that are important to your organization. The rest can vary from month to month, depending on answers to the first questions. If you discover a problem, ask additional questions in that area to focus on the details of the problem. Response to a typical paper survey is about 40%, but there are things you can do to improve the return. Tell patients the survey is coming, and ask them to complete it. Tell them again when they leave. Ask them whether they have responded when you have contact with them again. Share the collective results with the physicians, and ask them to reinforce compliance with their patients. Electronic or e-mail surveys are popular, but don't be afraid to sit with a pencil and tally paper surveys.

SUMMARY

That's it. You can make your quality management system as simple or as complex as you want. Certainly, accreditation standards such as TJC, AAAHC, or NIAHO can be included, as appropriate. The ISO standards provide the management structure to ensure that compliance with external standards happens, that employees have what they need to do a good job, and that patients and other customers are happy with the services they receive.

References

1. J. West, C. A. Cianfrani, and J. J. Tsiakals, "Standards outlook quality management principles: foundation of ISO 9000:2000 family," *Quality Progress* 33: 113–116, Feb. 2000.

2. M. Warnack, "Continual improvement programs and ISO 9001:2000," *Quality Progress* 36: 42–49, Mar. 2003.

3. J. Ketola and K. Roberts, "Demystifying ISO 9001:2000: Expanded section 6 resource management requirements cover worker competence, evaluation and training," *Quality Progress* 33: 65–70, Sept. 2000.

4. ISO, International Workshop Agreement: IWA 1, "Quality Management Systems—Guidelines for process improvements in health service organizations." IWA 1: 2001, Switzerland, 2001.

5. C. Cochran, "Document control made easy: ISO 9001:2000's mandates can be a blessing rather than a curse," *Quality Digest* 22: 29–35, June 2002.

6. American National Standards Institute, "Quality Management Systems—Requirements," American National Standard (ANSI/ISO/ASQ, Q9001–2008). Washington, D.C., 2000.

7. Jan Carlzon, *Moments of Truth* (New York, NY: Harper Collins, 1987).

3

Practical Aspects of Establishing a Quality Management System: How-to-do-it

Implementing an ISO 9001 QMS is a challenge for any organization, but it can be accomplished within a reasonable time frame by using an organized approach. Many organizations will find a consultant beneficial in working through the process; there are a number of consultants today who have had experience with quality systems in healthcare. Consultants can help in planning the implementation, suggesting formats for writing documents, conducting training in areas such as internal auditing, and assisting in preparation for external and registration audits. An implementation team must be formed as well, with the task of addressing the issues discussed in this chapter. This team should consist of both leadership and local champions from throughout the organization who will assist in developing the document system and writing policies, procedures, and work instructions and who will become internal auditors.

CHOOSING A REGISTRAR

The registrar is an independent company that is authorized to evaluate your organization and its capability to meet the ISO 9001 requirements. There are more than 70 registrars in the United States, but only a portion of these are experienced in healthcare registration. It is important to select one with healthcare experience. The registrar, which should be selected early in the process, will assist your organization in the following areas:

- Setting up a timetable for implementation and preparation
- Reviewing the quality manual prior to the audit
- Planning a pre-assessment visit to obtain feedback on whether the organization is ready for the formal audit
- Conducting the registration audit

- Working with your organization following the registration audit to address major issues and nonconformities that have been found

- Conducting surveillance audits at least annually and working with your organization over time to continually improve your QMS

MANAGEMENT/LEADERSHIP COMMITMENT

The ISO 9001 quality management system is a model for organizing a healthcare enterprise around sound management and business practices. As with most initiatives, success is dependent upon commitment from leadership and top management. Once a decision has been made to pursue ISO certification, commitment must be conveyed to the employees throughout the organization in order to clearly set the goals and expectations. This communication can be achieved by developing written documents, establishing blogs, utilizing website postings, and scheduling meetings. The following eight quality management principles of ISO 9001 must be communicated and discussed:

1. **Customer focus**—seeking to understand customer needs, meet their requirements, and exceed their expectations

2. **Leadership**—setting direction and developing a strategy in order to achieve the goals and objectives of the organization

3. **Involvement of people**—involving everyone in the organization and equipping each employee with the resources necessary to achieve the goals that are set

4. **Process approach**—achieving the desired results (outputs) by managing resources and services (inputs) as a process

5. **Systems approach to management**—improving an organization's effectiveness by understanding and managing interrelated processes for a given objective

6. **Continual improvement**—focusing on improvement as a permanent objective of the organization

7. **Factual approach to decision making**—using data and information to make effective and informed decisions

8. **Mutually beneficial supplier relationships**—developing relationships that are mutually beneficial and create value for everyone involved

Within the context of these principles, management should explain the specific reasons for pursuing certification and emphasize the goals of improving patient/customer satisfaction and efficiency while reducing costs and errors. An important point is to assure employees that they will be involved in developing the QMS by helping to write and review policies, procedures, and work instructions. The purpose, in many instances, is to understand and clearly describe how work and processes are being performed; employees should not view the ISO QMS implementation as a threat to their jobs.

At this time it may be helpful to conduct a gap analysis to determine whether elements in the organization are absent or not adequate according to the ISO standard. Furthermore, the method through which these elements are addressed must comply with the ISO standard. A consultant is often helpful in this process. Typical findings of a gap analysis include inadequate work instructions, lack of follow-up on corrective action plans, improper statistical methods, and outdated supplies or medications.

WRITING A QUALITY POLICY, MANUAL, AND OBJECTIVES

The next step is to establish a quality policy, create quality objectives, and write a quality manual for the organization. The quality policy can be the same as the mission statement of the organization, although it does not have to be. In general, a mission statement should describe how the organization plans to achieve its vision. For example, Google's mission is "to organize the world's information and make it universally accessible and useful." Amazon's mission statement is "to build a place where people can come to find and discover anything they might want to buy online." The quality policy, however, should be more directed toward quality issues. For example, "ensuring that the information collected by our proprietary software system is accurate and timely."

Quality objectives should also be clear and concise. At Physicians' Clinic of Iowa, the objectives are:

- To maintain a high level of satisfaction for our patients and other customers
- To contain costs for both patients and the hospitals we serve
- To return our patients to active lives with maximal functional capacity
- To monitor clinical outcomes on a regular basis in order to make continued improvements in patient care
- To continually assess issues regarding patient safety in order to ensure patient well-being and reduce errors

After writing the quality policy and quality objectives, attention is directed to writing the quality manual. This requires studying ANSI/ISO/ASQ Q9001–2008: *Quality management systems—Requirements*. The quality manual describes the organization's quality system and is the starting point for the auditing process. It explains what the organization is trying to accomplish and how the quality system functions within the organization. A designated individual manager or group should study the standard and rewrite every clause and subclause in their own words, adjusting for the organization's goals and objectives within the context of the standard and its requirements. When completed, there will be 60–70 short policy statements describing *what* the organization is doing and what it intends to achieve. The statements should be written in plain English so that everyone in the organization can understand them. The subsequent steps will focus on understanding the key processes and then describing their importance so that the QMS essentially shows *how* the organization will achieve its goals and objectives. This process entails writing procedures, which is described in the next section.

IDENTIFYING AND MAPPING KEY PROCESSES

At this point, the key processes of the organization should be identified. The process approach is fundamental to the ISO 9001 QMS; identifying and mapping or flowcharting key processes is helpful for many reasons. Recall that a process is any set of associated activities that have inputs and generate outputs. Most organizations have 5 to 10 key processes and a variety of supporting processes. Examples of healthcare service delivery and support processes are illustrated in Table 3.1 and Table 3.2. Each process is matched with the corresponding quality objective(s) of the organization, followed by the key requirements for the process and the performance measurements used to monitor the process.

After indentifying and defining a key process within the context of the quality objectives of the organization, it is often helpful to map or flowchart the process. Not all processes require mapping, but more complex multi-step processes should be mapped to allow people to understand the flow of work and where documents fit within the process steps. For example, in Figures 3.1 and 3.2, the steps in the clinical patient flow process have been mapped from the point of referral to a specialist office to the point of performance of imaging studies. Although many other steps are subsequently involved in the entire process, these figures illustrate patient flow and work flow and show that there are documents supporting some of the steps (shown on the right with designated numbers). For example: In Figure 3.1, when the appointment is arranged the supporting document is Appointment Process 3501PCI. Patient and family education are described in Patient/Family Education 5502PCI (Figure 3.2). By having a controlled document system aligned with process maps of key processes, the process maps are easier to read, contain less clutter, and direct the reader to appropriate supporting documents.

Table 3.1 Healthcare service delivery processes.

Process	Quality Objectives	Key Requirements	Performance Mesurements
Physician Staff • Provider evaluation • Surgical/medical patient care process • Provider service delivery	• Clinical outcomes • Clinical process • Customer satisfaction • Functional outcomes • Patient safety	• Recognition for quality care • Development of clinical protocols • Professionalism	• Peri-operative antibiotic timing • Peri-operative antibiotic type • Peri-operative antibiotic duration • Surgical site infection rate • Patient satisfaction survey
Clinical Staff • Clinical staff preparation • Appointment scheduling • Registration • Care management plan • Surgical/medical patient care process	• Clinical outcomes • Clinical process • Customer satisfaction • Functional outcomes • Patient safety	• Accuracy • Compassion • Efficiency • Professionalism	• Patient satisfaction survey • Training/ competency records • Chart documentation
Education • Patient/family education	• Clinical process • Customer satisfaction	• Informed customers	• Chart documentation
Health Promotion • Patient/family education	• Customer satisfaction	• Promotion of community health	Participation: • Breast cancer walk • Prostate screening • American Heart Association heart walk

Table 3.2 Healthcare support processes.

Process	Quality Objectives	Key Requirements	Performance Mesurements
Accounting/Revenue	• Cost containment • Customer satisfaction	• Accuracy • Timeliness	• Days in AR (accounts receivable) • % aging • Profile reports • Monthly financial statements
Compliance	• Clinical outcomes • Patient safety	• Accuracy • Practice within legal guidelines	• Chart audits • OSHA audits • CLIA audits
Human Resources	• Customer satisfaction	• Trained and competent staff	• Employee turnover • Employee satisfaction
Information Services	• Customer satisfaction	• Availability • Speed	• Disk space • Virus checks
Management	• Cost containment • Customer satisfaction • Patient safety	• Budget planning • Management review	• Monthly financial statements • Audit reports • Corrective–preventive action reports • Customer feedback
Marketing	• Customer satisfaction	• Service	• Community sponsorship • Referral provider survey
Relationship with Partners (PHO, Hospitals, ASU)	• Clinical outcomes • Cost containment • Customer satisfaction	• Open communication • Product quality	• Supplier evaluations • ASU financial report • Data collection • Committee reports • CR PHO monthly update
Risk Management	• Customer satisfaction • Patient safety	• Minimal errors	• Patient comment form • Patient comment log • Patient satisfaction survey • Liability case evaluation • Annual risk assessment

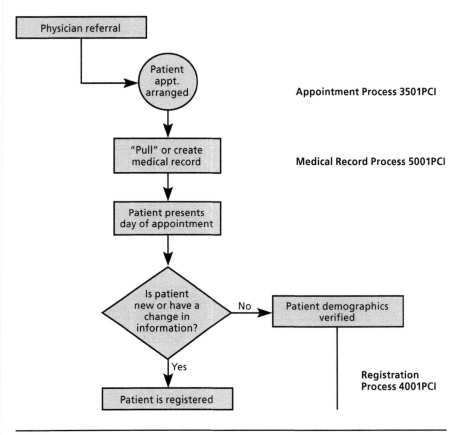

Figure 3.1 Clinical patient flow, process 1.

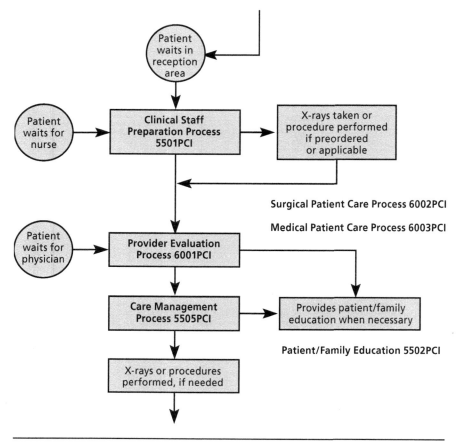

Figure 3.2 Clinical patient flow, process 2.

ESTABLISHING A CONTROLLED DOCUMENT SYSTEM

A controlled document system is another major feature of implementing a QMS. After writing the quality manual, creating a controlled document system is the second milestone in implementation. The idea behind a controlled document system is that all documents should be in the same format with a clear title, scope (purpose), and supporting and linked records that show who approved the document and any revisions that have been made. Using this system, all employees are assured that documents are available, current, and correct within the context of the QMS. Examples from Physicians' Clinic of Iowa are shown in Figures 3.3 and 3.4. One important point is that all documents are in the same format and easily recognizable.

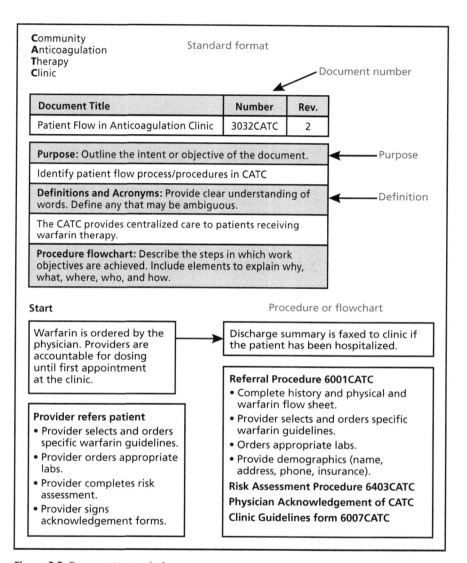

Figure 3.3 Document example 1.

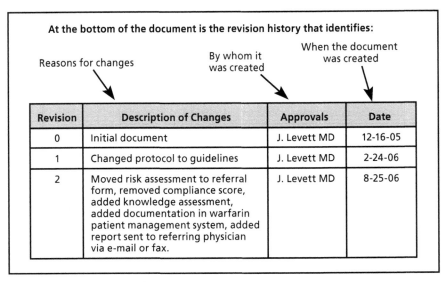

At the bottom of the document is the revision history that identifies:

Reasons for changes

By whom it was created

When the document was created

Revision	Description of Changes	Approvals	Date
0	Initial document	J. Levett MD	12-16-05
1	Changed protocol to guidelines	J. Levett MD	2-24-06
2	Moved risk assessment to referral form, removed compliance score, added knowledge assessment, added documentation in warfarin patient management system, added report sent to referring physician via e-mail or fax.	J. Levett MD	8-25-06

Figure 3.4 Document example 2.

Figure 3.5 depicts the components of a controlled document system. The system is best understood by thinking of the quality manual as the statement of the policies of the organization. These policies are supported by written procedures, often described using flowcharts. In many instances, work instructions are written to provide detailed "how-to" instructions to accomplish a task. They are unique to each department and are controlled by the department. These instructions should be clear and concise. They may be a narrative, flowchart, pictures, or drawings—anything that helps to clearly communicate the instructions is appropriate. Information that is gathered as the result of a transaction with a customer becomes a record. In general, documents such as procedures or work instructions are paperwork that can be revised; they are not records. Records, then, are legal documents that cannot be revised.

Establishing a controlled document system requires a review of all current documents within the organization. This work reveals outdated and duplicated documents and highlights the need to write new documents in order to comply with the standard. Six required procedures for ISO 9001:2008 must be written:

- Document Control (clause 4.2.3)
- Control of Quality Records (clause 4.2.4)
- Internal Audit (clause 8.2.2)
- Control of Nonconformity (clause 8.3)
- Corrective Action (clause 8.5.2)
- Preventive Action (clause 8.5.3)

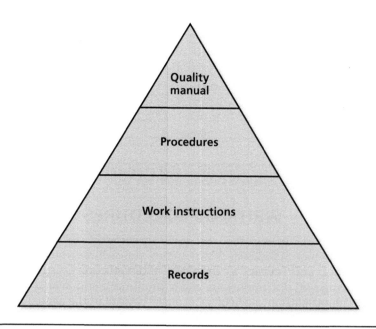

Figure 3.5 Components of a controlled document system.

It is necessary to establish a clear numbering system for all documents. This system can be numeric or alphanumeric. For example, at Physicians' Clinic of Iowa (PCI), each document created for the quality management system is numbered according to the following system. The number identifies the area or type of information and alpha characters identify the location where the process is used.

1. A number is assigned to each area of the approved quality system documentation:

Administration	1000	Surgery Scheduling	6500
Accounting	1500	Business Office	7000
Human Resources	2000	Laboratory	7500
Quality Improvement	2500	Diagnostic Testing	8000
Quality System	3000	a. Radiology	8100
Appointment	3500	b. Audiology	8200
Reception	4000	c. Neuro Studies	8300
Registration	4500	d. EKG	8400
Medical Records	5000	Marketing	8500
Nursing	5500	Information Services	9000
Physician	6000	OSHA	9500

2. An alpha or letter set is assigned to each location. The PCI label appears on documents pertaining to all locations. A site-specific alpha is assigned to processes designated for a specific location.

All Locations	PCI	Rheumatology	RHM
Otolaryngology	ENT	Surgical Specialists	SS
Neurology	NEU	Urology	URO
Orthopaedics	ORT		

3. When a document pertains to a specific physician, the assigned practice management system number will follow the alpha.

WRITING PROCEDURES

Procedures must be written. As noted previously, six procedures are required by ISO 9001:2008. Many other procedures must be written, consolidated, and revised as the QMS is developed. Using a standardized structure, all documents are easily monitored and available, and can be understood without difficulty because they are in the same format.

A few rules regarding procedure writing are worth noting. To determine whether a procedure should be written, ask the following questions:

- Is it something done every day by more than one person? If so, it is probably not necessary to write the procedure. If it is a task performed infrequently or one that is hard to remember, it probably should be written down.

- Is there only one person trained to do the job? If so, procedures should be written and key steps clearly stated.

Remember that written procedures are for trained employees, not unqualified individuals. Do not be too wordy or overly detailed; flowcharts work well. Procedures must have a clearly stated purpose, a clear beginning, and a clear ending. Remember that it is only necessary to document the aspects of a process or procedure that are subject to error, misunderstanding, or misinterpretation. A few ground rules that may be helpful:

- Ask "What am I trying to say?"

- Make the meaning very clear.

- Sift out irrelevant material.

- Use understandable language and correct grammar.

- Avoid jargon and obscure acronyms.

- Use simple language to convey the thought and utilize short sentences. Pictures and diagrams are often useful.

- Use clear words and phrases. Separate ideas into individual sentences or paragraphs.

AUDITING

Both internal and external auditing are important requirements of an ISO 9001 QMS. External auditing is performed by the registrar on an annual basis; internal auditing is done during the year by employees who have been trained as auditors. Internal auditor training is another milestone in ISO implementation. It is an opportunity for employees to participate in the ISO process. Through becoming an auditor, many employees will have a "now I get it" experience. Training should be provided by an experienced auditor who has a training background. Employees from throughout the organization should be given the opportunity to participate in the training.

STAFF AND PHYSICIAN INVOLVEMENT AND EDUCATION

Staff are, of course, involved in auditor training and in reviewing and writing procedures as the controlled document system is developed. It is important to understand that the QMS is only useful when it utilizes input from the people who perform the processes on a daily basis— everyone must participate in order to be successful. The implementation must be presented to employees as a way to structure workflow and organize their processes, not as a threat to their jobs. Physicians must understand that having a QMS in place will make their work easier and the work of the staff more structured and dependable and less variable. At PCI, monthly newsletters were written during the implementation process. An example is included here:

> We have been working almost two years to establish the ISO 9001 Quality Management System within PCI. In order to successfully implement this system, it is important that all employees, including physicians, be aware of the features and able to describe the important concepts of the management system.
>
> We have enclosed several documents for your review:
>
> - A list of the PCI quality objectives. Please read and familiarize yourself with these objectives.
>
> - A matrix of responsibility for the quality management system. Physicians are required to be aware of and to be knowledgeable of certain elements that relate to the process of care.

PCI matrix of responsibility.

ISO 9001:2008 Requirement		Nursing	Physician
4	**Quality Management System**		
4.1	General Requirements	Aware	Aware
4.2	Documentation Requirements	Aware	Aware
4.2.1	General	Aware	Aware
4.2.2	Quality Manual	Aware	Aware
4.2.3	Control of Documents	Aware	Aware
4.2.4	Control of Records	Aware	Aware
5	**Management Responsibility**		
5.1	Management Commitment	Aware	Owner/Aware
5.2	Patient/Customer Focus	Aware	Aware
5.3	Quality Policy	Know	Know
5.4	Planning	Aware	Aware
5.4.1	Quality Objectives	Know	Know
5.4.2	Quality Management System Planning	Aware	Aware
5.5.1	Responsibility and Authority	Aware	Aware
5.5.2	Management Representative	Aware	Aware
5.5.3	Internal Communication	Know	Know
5.6	Management Review	Aware	Aware
6	**Resource Management**		
6.1	Provision of Resources	Aware	Aware
6.2	Human Resources	Aware	Aware
6.3	Infrastructure	Aware	Aware
6.4	Work Environment	Process	Process
7	**Service Realization**		
7.1	Planning of Service Realization	Process	Process
7.2	Patient/Customer-related Processes	Process	Process
7.2.1	Determination of Requirements Related to Service	Process	Process
7.2.2	Review of Requirements Related to Service	Process	Process
7.2.3	Patient/Customer Communication	Process	Aware
7.3	Design and Development *(Note: Design and development may be excluded in many healthcare organizations.*		
7.4	Purchasing	Aware	Aware
7.4.1	Purchasing Process	Process	Aware
7.4.2	Purchasing Information	Process	Aware
7.4.3	Verification of Purchased Product	Process	Aware

(Continued)

PCI matrix of responsibility.   *(Continued)*

ISO 9001:2008 Requirement	Nursing	Physician
7.5 Service Provision	Process	Process
7.5.1 Control of Service Provision	Process	Process
7.5.2 Validation of Processes for Service Provision	Process	Process
7.5.3 Identification and Traceability	Process	Process
7.5.4 Patient/Customer Property	Process	Aware
7.5.5 Preservation of Product	Process	Aware
7.6 Control of Monitoring and Measuring Devices	Aware	Aware
8 **Measurement, Analysis, Improvements**		
8.1 General	Aware	Aware
8.2.1 Patient/Customer Satisfaction	Process	Process
8.2.2 Internal Audit	Aware	Aware
8.2.3 Monitoring and Measurement of Processes	Aware	Aware
8.2.4 Monitoring and Measurement of Service	Process	Process
8.3 Control of Nonconforming Service	Process	Aware
8.4 Analysis of Data	Aware	Aware
8.5 Improvement	Owner	Owner
8.5.1 Continual Improvement	Owner	Owner
8.5.2 Corrective Action	Aware	Aware
8.5.3 Preventive Action	Aware	Aware

We will be providing all physicians and practice managers with a copy of a quality manual that has been written and revised several times as we have moved through the ISO 9001 accreditation process.

With respect to physicians, it is extremely important to involve them early in the ISO implementation process. Communication methods must be developed involving a combination of e-mails, paper memos, blogs, and more. When we implemented ISO 9001 at Physicians' Clinic of Iowa several years ago, we used bimonthly newsletters over the course of the 2.5 years we took to become certified to ISO 9001. Because some physicians preferred to read e-mails and others preferred paper memos, we found a combination of e-mails and paper memos to be an effective communication technique. Examples of some key information messages we sent to the physicians are included here:

What is the PCI quality policy?

The PCI quality policy is the mission statement of the organization:

The Physicians' Clinic of Iowa, P.C. is a physician-owned and physician-governed multi-specialty group whose mission is to deliver the highest quality of multi-specialty healthcare to individual patients in eastern Iowa. We will coordinate this care to be a value to our patients and other purchasers of healthcare. We are committed to comply with the requirements of and continually improve the quality of healthcare for our patients.

Is it important that PCI employees and physicians be knowledgeable about the quality management system (QMS).

We are working together to provide the best possible care to our patients, and it is important to know that the ISO 9001 quality management system is in place to support us in providing this care. Quality management principles, on which ISO 9001 is based, have been adopted from many highly successful and effective organizations.

How do we ensure that the QMS is, in fact, appropriately deployed and used throughout the organization?

Both internal and external audits are used to ensure that the QMS is appropriately understood and utilized. A number of PCI employees have undergone internal auditor training, and we have completed two internal audits within all of the departments at PCI. It is important to know that the audits will continue on a regular basis throughout the year. In order to obtain formal registration, an external audit will be performed in a few months. Physicians, as well as other employees, may be asked questions by the auditors; therefore, it is important that everyone be knowledgeable about the QMS.

Will auditors be questioning PCI physicians about the QMS?

PCI physicians may be questioned by the auditors. The information provided in these newsletters will provide PCI physicians with sufficient knowledge to answer most questions. If a physician is unsure of a process-type question, it would be appropriate to refer to the quality document notebook before answering a question.

What is the PCI quality document notebook?

Each department has a copy of the PCI quality document note-book, which contains up-to-date records of all documents used throughout the organization. Everyone should be aware of the location of the notebook and review the table of contents.

Does PCI have flowcharts that describe patient care in the office?

Physicians should be aware that the general patient care flowchart (3032PCI) describes the flow of the patient through PCI. Two other flowcharts describe the surgical and medical patient care processes (6002 PCI; 6003PCI). These flowcharts are contained in the PCI quality document notebook.

How are customer complaints handled at PCI?

PCI has both a customer complaint process (3008PCI) and a comment form (3009PCI), which are available for customer complaints. PCI also has a policy for lost or damaged patient property (3033PCI).

What are the eight quality management principles that ISO 9001 is based upon?

The eight quality management principles of ISO 9001 are:

- Customer focus
- Leadership
- Involvement of people
- Process approach
- System approach to management
- Continual improvement
- Factual approach to decision making
- Mutually beneficial supplier relationships

4

ISO and the Culture of a Healthcare Organization

The term *culture* refers to a population or group of people and includes values, habits, ideals, and sometimes religious beliefs. Often there are subcultures within a group, so we talk about a Southern culture, a New England culture, or a Southwestern culture within the framework of an American culture. In describing a cultural group, social psychologists often refer to three aspects of culture:

1. The basic belief system, often unconscious and developed over time. Sometimes referred to as "home training."

2. The espoused beliefs or declared values. "I pledge allegiance to the flag…"

3. Evidence of how the culture has behaved, particularly in times of stress.

Although there is no universally agreed upon system for evaluating a culture, this system will give a fair picture.

In a similar manner, it is possible to assess an organization's culture to describe various aspects of it and thus understand how things are done there and what kind of place it is to work. The task is a bit more complex, however, because each organization exists within a broader culture, and each employee brings personal beliefs as well as cultural baggage from prior employers.

There is thus another aspect of organizational culture that influences quality efforts—the strength of the culture itself. If the corporate culture is weak, the organization will not behave as a cohesive unit and reactions to stress are unpredictable. Customers may not get the same predictable service. In this setting, it is difficult or impossible to introduce culture change or a new management system. It's hard to steer the ship when you can't find the rudder.

On the other hand, a strong, new CEO may have an easier time in such an organization, because there is no existing culture to overcome as he seeks to introduce change.

With a strong existing culture, there is a dichotomy between a situation in which employees salute the chief because he is the chief and one in which the CEO has inspired employees to believe in his system. The difference is in the level of commitment among the employees. Peter Senge[1] talks about a learning organization in which improvement transcends individual achievement. Early in the first year of a new surgery center, employees reported in a survey that they thought the quality of their individual performance was "excellent" but that the quality of service by the center as a whole was only "good." One year later, the answers to those questions were reversed. Employees now rated the quality of the service by the center as better than their own individual performance. They had learned to work together to move the center toward truly excellent service. Learning and improvement had become part of the organization's culture.

ASSESSING THE CULTURE
OF THE ORGANIZATION[2]

First, the CEO. Do employees know him? Have they ever seen him? Is his presence felt? I remember walking up to a hospital information desk and asking directions to "the office of the CEO, Mr. James Green." The response was, "James who?" Many CEOs prefer to manage behind closed doors. They see themselves as making important decisions that affect the corporation and just don't have time to chat with employees. Some are uncomfortable in a public role. By contrast, I knew a hospital CEO who started each day on the top floor and passed thru every nursing station on the way to his office—management by walking around.

Different strokes. It's not that one style is superior, but the strategy for introducing an ISO 9001 management system will be different in different cultures. It would be unfair to ask the first CEO to engage in a public advocacy program. He can make the decision and secure the funds, but someone else must be the spokesperson. By the same token, it would be unfair to paste responsibility for a public campaign into the second CEO's schedule. He's already there. He should spend his time doing other things.

Another aspect of culture is the ability to control budgets and spend money. Are spending decisions made by a small group at the top or do front line employees have the ability to spend money to improve their process? Ask employees how far up the org chart they would have to go for permission to spend $10,000. Two levels is risky. More than that means decisions are likely made by people who don't really know what's going on. The Ritz Carlton hotels once had a policy that any employee could spend up to $2,000 to solve a guest problem. Someone asked their spokesman if that policy was ever abused, and the answer was, "Yes, but not often." Ritz Carlton tolerated the occasional misapplication of funds in exchange for the greater good of solving guest problems instantly. A California hospital adopted a similar policy and allowed any nursing units to spend up to $10,000 to improve patient care. In the first two years, the money spent was less than the amount budgeted.

What does that say about culture? If you have an idea to improve the process where you work, does anyone care? If an individual has an idea for improving the quality of services provided by the organization, is there a mechanism to get that idea up to a person who can evaluate and implement it? All this is similar conceptually to the AHRQ survey of patient safety (http://www.ahrq.gov/qual/patientsafetyculture/mosurv index.htm). If you have an idea to improve patient safety, is anyone listening? The concept of a "safety culture"[3] implies that safety has become more than a stated goal or "a good idea." It is an intuitive part of every employee's thinking and supported by every level of management.

One of the key tenets of employee empowerment is that employees must be allowed to be wrong. No one will implement an idea if it's necessary to be right all the time. The same principle applies to raising children. If you make all the decisions for them, they never learn to decide for themselves. They must be allowed to make mistakes and suffer the consequences, as long as there is a safety net that they can't see.

A related question has to do with how dissent is handled. Employees will resist change. Everyone resists change! Residents near my home objected vociferously when the county wanted to pave the gravel road in front of their houses. When you announce that you will institute an ISO 9001 management system, most employees will resist. The following quote from Machiavelli highlights the natural resistance to change of any sort:

> *It must be realized that there is nothing more difficult to plan, more uncertain of success, or more dangerous to manage than the establishment of a new order of government: for he who introduces it makes enemies of all those who derived advantages from the old order and finds but lukewarm defenders among those who stand to gain from the new one.*
>
> *Such a lukewarm attitude grows partly out of fear of the adversaries, who have the law on their side, and partly from the incredulity of men in general, who actually have no faith in new things until they have been proven by experience.*

From: *The Prince* by N. Machiavelli, 1513.

Some employees are, by nature, disgruntled and unhappy. They will oppose anything management wants to do. Fellow employees will not tolerate or embrace dissent from these sources as long as there is a credible alternative. If management provides a reasonable explanation of the proposed "new order," this irrational, instinctive dissent will not prosper. However, reasonable, questioning dissent must be addressed, lest it become creative dissent. A question—especially one with a small element of truth—may become the nidus, a nest or breeding place, of a false construct if it is not dealt with promptly. The bigger the lie, or the more often repeated, the more likely it will be believed. Political campaigns use this axiom often.

Finally, there is communication. Do employees know what is going on with the organization? What's the bottom line? What are the greatest threats? Most important, do they *feel* informed? Do employees believe that senior management communicates with them on a regular basis? And turn this around. Does anyone listen? Is there a forum or mechanism employees can use to communicate with management above their level?

Secretary of State Hillary Clinton regularly holds town meetings in a large auditorium, where State Department employees may ask uncensored questions. Not all concern foreign policy, but she responds to each. There is also an "ASK" button on the internal web site, and questions posed there do get answered.

I worked in an organization once where the suggestion box was never used. Employees were afraid they would be fired if they expressed an idea that was counter to the conventional wisdom. No one had ever actually been fired, and it was legally not possible to dismiss an employee without due process, but many feared they might be the first. This was a culture of fear and intimidation.

In another organization, the suggestion box was never used because it was unnecessary. "If I have an idea, I just tell my supervisor, and it's done. Why should I write it down?"

If you want to evaluate your organization's culture, answer the following questions. Note that there is no numerical score. No points. This is a subjective assessment, but it will give you a picture that will have implications for implementing ISO or any dramatic change in the organization. Be careful. Whatever your perspective—top management or front line employee—your opinion may not give an accurate representation of the organization as a whole. Surveys, focus groups, and/or outside consultants may be required to obtain a balanced, accurate picture.

Role of the Individual

Are employees regarded as cogs in the machinery (and thus easily replaced) or as respected partners in providing service? The question is: How do employees feel about this?

Power

Who makes decisions, and how broadly based is the advisory group? The CEO is responsible for all the decisions, but how willing is he to consider contrary opinions? At the other extreme is the organization without central authority, where decisions are made by local units.

Communication

Does everyone in the organization know what's going on everywhere else, or is information shared only on a "need to know" basis? As always, it's important to ask how employees feel about this issue.

Strength

Assess the strength of whatever culture you have. One good way to do this is to look for consistency in answers to questions such as "How would your company react to a crisis?"

As with any subjective assessment, there are no absolutes and there may be many sub-issues. However, a thorough evaluation of these elements will give you an overall view of the culture in your organization and help you evaluate the implications for adoption of ISO 9001.

CULTURE AND STRATEGY

Culture will influence implementation strategy,[4] although it's not all or none. Whatever the culture, it will probably be necessary to do some of everything; your culture will influence where you spend most of your time or money. Support from the top is important for any change. In an organization with a strong leader and central authority, repetitive public endorsement by the CEO will be essential to provide credibility. On the other hand, in an organization where decisions are made by individual process owners rather than a central authority figure, more efforts should be made at lower levels in the organization to gain broad acceptance of the new system.

Overcoming resistance will always be a problem. Books have been written about change management, and introducing the ISO 9001 quality management system is a form of organizational change. Here are some strategies that have proven useful for the authors:

1. **Keep it simple.** Focus on a few key elements of ISO that are easy to remember and have visible benefits. For example, customer focus, metrics, and document control.

2. **Make it easy.** Initially, many employees will have difficulty with document control and with deciding what to measure or how to present data. Have experts available to assist with these tasks, particularly in the first few months.

3. **Training.** Extend the understanding of ISO both horizontally and vertically within the organization. At least one member of each process team should have had formal training in ISO principles.

4. **Audits.** Internal audits introduce a bit of peer pressure and benefit the auditors as well as the auditees by enhancing their understanding of other processes in the organization. External audits provide independent assessments and give employees a chance to demonstrate excellence. At the State Department, we have an award for outstanding performance on triennial external audits.

5. **Management reviews.** Any weak areas are immediately obvious to the managers in charge of those areas. Share minutes of these reviews with all employees, and don't forget to point out instances of excellence.

6. **Share success.** The minutes of the management review meetings should include charts of process and outcome metrics in addition to surveys or other input from customers. Even failure can indicate success. When one process in our system failed to meet goals, this was clearly shown to be due to a surge in demand that swamped capacity. As a result of this presentation at management review, additional resources were provided. This was a failure within the process, but a successful application of management review.

The initiation of an ISO 9001 quality management system may serve as a tool for instilling a culture of quality in an organization. The standards call for measuring customer satisfaction and continual improvement, thus inspiring employees to seek ways to constantly improve what they do. At first, this may be done in response to requirements. Eventually, however, it becomes a habit and part of the organization's culture.

SUMMARY

Although similar problems are encountered with any change, the intrinsic culture of the organization will influence how those problems are solved. Remain focused on the eventual goal of making ISO part of the culture. "This is the way we do things here."

References

1. P. M. Senge, The Fifth Discipline: *The art and practice of the learning organization* (London: Random House, 1990).

2. www.infed.org/thinkers/senge.htm

3. V. F. Nieva and J. Sorra, "Safety Culture assessment: a tool for improving patient safety in healthcare organizations," *Quality and Safety in Health Care:* 12(Suppl II): ii17–ii23, 2003.

4. R. I. Ababaneh, "The role of organizational culture on practicing quality improvement in Jordanian public hospitals," *Leadership in Health Services:* 244–259, 2010.

5

Incorporating Quality Tools and Techniques into an ISO QMS

ISO AND OTHER SYSTEMS

One of the advantages of ISO as a management system is its versatility in accommodating other tools and techniques. There are requirements in ISO to identify and address problems and to make improvement. However, the mechanism for accomplishing those tasks is left as an exercise for the user. Thus the organization is not obligated to use any single tool in solving all problems but is free to utilize whatever tool is appropriate for the problem at hand. No special certifications or training are required by the QMS for the solution of problems. Simple problems can employ simple solutions. It is important to distinguish a high-level management system that sits like an umbrella over the entire organization from tools and techniques that can be deployed locally to solve problems.

Indeed, papers have come from constituents of The Joint Commission (TJC), the Baldrige Award, and even ISO 9001 demonstrating links and similarities between their systems. It might be expected that with periodic changes in the various systems of standards, they would grow to resemble one another. Good ideas are quickly imitated, and one way to confront competition in the world of standards is to say, "We offer that too!"

Another significant difference between the ISO quality management system and other standards, such as TJC, is stability. TJC standards are revised every year and new standards are written for new issues that surface in the healthcare policy arena. The ISO standards are written for a broader audience, and revisions are less frequent and directed more toward clarification of issues. The basic concepts and requirements in ISO don't change from year to year. There is, of course, nothing to prevent the organization from addressing a current issue, such as patient safety, but they are free to adopt solutions that fit their setting or satisfy external requirements.

INCORPORATING TOOLS

An organization may require that a given tool be used in certain situations, but there is no specific requirement in the ISO standards to do so. The State Department (DOS), for example, requires a root cause analysis (RCA) when health units report a patient complaint, death, or adverse event. When reporting an adverse event, it is not sufficient to say, "The nurse made a mistake." We want to know why the nurse made that mistake and what you have done to ensure that it doesn't happen again. A procedure for handling adverse events was required by ISO 9001 standard 8.5.2, and we chose to include root cause analysis as a requirement in that policy. The elements of a root cause analysis were incorporated into the form used to report these events to reinforce the adoption of this approach to a solution.

The Department of State has roughly 180 separate locations where errors can be made; prior to ISO, the response to an error was, "We'll be more careful next time." Obviously, without a viable systematic approach, working harder was not a successful strategy. In addition, other locations never knew the circumstances that led to the error, so they were destined to repeat it. After our requirement for RCA, we discovered several problems that were present almost everywhere:

1. There was no defined protocol for giving immunizations. As a result, protocols existed only in the minds of individual nurses. Most of these usually worked, but they were occasionally extended into unusual situations where they did not work.

2. Our recording procedure for immunizations did not include a universal location or form for recording immunizations at every location. When patients moved to a new location, their charts contained different forms located at different places in the chart, and records of prior immunizations were occasionally missed. The result was duplicate immunizations and a loss of confidence by the patients in that health unit.

3. Being "busy" was frequently mentioned as a contributing factor to immunization errors. Drilling down to the causes for "busy" revealed several correctable situations:

    a. Over-scheduling. Nurses tried to accommodate patients who should have been asked to return at a less busy time. In one case, the nurse was giving a shot to one patient while talking to the next patient about her immunizations.

    b. Noise. All patients—adults and children—were in the same exam room at the same time with one nurse.

    c. Lack of training or experience. When the nurse was busy, the doctor stepped in to give shots—and did it incorrectly, because he was not accustomed to doing this.

The ISO requirement for management review is similar in some ways to the "balanced scorecard" concept, and a balanced scorecard may be used under the ISO umbrella (http://en.wikipedia.org/wiki/Balanced_scorecard). However, the flexibility of ISO allows for a selection by process owners of the parameters to be reported, subject to feedback from senior management. The balanced scorecard concept requires metrics on specific areas (financial, processes, customers, personnel, and so on) from various parts of the organization. These could be included in the management review process specified under ISO 9001. However, ISO would also allow custom metrics from each section, depending on what is appropriate or desired. For example, our sections that deal broadly with DOS employees or the public are asked to report more extensively on customer needs and satisfaction. Certainly other sections have internal customers who are also important, but these may not be critically important within a particular section.

THE MALCOLM BALDRIGE NATIONAL QUALITY AWARD

The Malcolm Baldrige National Quality Award was originally developed to discover and promote excellence in American business. The intent was to identify a few examples of excellence in various types of businesses so that these practices could be emulated broadly in the American business community. The "Criteria for Performance Excellence" are widely used and have been progressively expanded to include awards in many segments of American industry, including healthcare, education, and government. Nothing in the Baldrige Criteria prevents their incorporation within an ISO management system, although the goals of the two programs are different. For example, the ISO standard for Human Resources (6.2) requires that employees "shall be competent on the basis of appropriate education, training, skills, and experience." The standard goes on to require the organization to provide the appropriate infrastructure and a work environment to allow employees to perform their tasks. Details on how this will be accomplished are left to the organization to specify.

The Baldrige Award Healthcare Criteria talk about Workforce Engagement (enrichment, development, and assessment) and Workforce Environment (capability and capacity, and climate). If these concepts are meaningful to the organization, they may be included in policies or procedures written to address ISO standard 6.2.

For example, at the State Department, we have a "competence assessment" form to be completed annually for every nurse in our overseas health units. Some of the items are status updates (license, BLS card) and some are required training (security, privacy). The task of the supervisor is to document completion and ensure that employees have opportunities to complete the required items. This may mean allocating time or money, but the annual checklist is a reminder to ensure the competence of employees in their section.

There is another important advantage to adopting internal policies rather than more complex external standards, and that is buy-in. Policies written internally are more likely to become part of the organization's culture—adopted and used because employees believe they are important, rather than because an external standards body dictates their adoption.

Another problem with external standards is that no standards-setting body can keep up with current thinking on a given subject frequently enough to encompass all that is good without creating a huge administrative burden. TJC, for example, issued a 20-page document on patient safety in July 2010, which did not mention the idea of using a checklist.

LEAN

The concept of Lean manufacturing and services is a cornerstone of the Toyota Production System and has been used by many businesses to improve the efficiency of their processes. Let's look at an example of how some Lean principles might be applied in an ambulatory surgery center (ASC) that is registered to ISO 9001. Table 5.1 lists seven classic types of waste for any process.

Table 5.1 Seven types of waste.

Waste type	Description
1. Overproduction	Providing a service no one wants
2. Waiting	Not having people, supplies, or equipment that you need
3. Transport	Moving people or things without purpose
4. Inventory	Having too much stuff – excess supplies
5. Processing	"Push" instead of "pull"
6. Motion	Motion that does not add value for the customer
7. Defects	Mistakes or variation

For healthcare, or more specifically for our ASC, here's what this means:

1. **Overproduction.** This concept was developed for manufacturing and referred to making more widgets than you could sell. For service industries such as healthcare, the thinking must be modified a bit. Services must be consumed when they are provided. Anything else is waste. In one sense, this refers to the capability to provide the service. If you staff four operating rooms (ORs) but only use three, the fourth room is overproduction.

2. **Waiting.** When a needed instrument or supply item is not available in the OR, there is a delay while someone goes to get it. To eliminate this wait in the future, the OR nurse who leaves the room documents the reason and that item is added to the kit for that operation next time. Another delay is associated with starting cases on time. Studies have shown that the most common reason surgery does not start on time is that the surgeon is not there. The reason surgeons came late was that the OR was commonly not ready. The ASC concentrated on having their ORs ready, and the surgeons began coming on time.

3. **Transport.** The neatnick's mantra is, "When you pick something up, don't put it down until you find its home." This relates to another Lean principle of keeping a neat workspace. In the ASC, all supplies are brought to a single, common supply room. There are no supply cupboards in the ORs. Supplies needed for a given operation are brought from the supply room to the OR. Anything not used is returned to supply at the end of the day.

4. **Inventory.** As part of the annual physical inventory, every item in every room, cart, or cupboard is priced. Then, we calculate the interest on the money needed to purchase all that stuff. This exercise makes believers out of employees whose bonus is linked to profits. There is also a time cost of having more than you need. When you are looking for something, all that other stuff has to be moved to find it.

5. **Processing.** Originally, patients who finished registering were "pushed" to the pre-op area to change clothes and wait for the OR. Now, they return to the waiting room until the OR signals it's time for the pre-op nurse to begin her 30-minute process. The pre-op area is less comfortable for the patient and more expensive for the ASC because of the more intense nursing care provided. Everybody wins by waiting for the surgery process to "pull" the patient along.

6. **Motion.** Commercial medical procedure kits are arranged so the user doesn't have to rearrange the contents before performing the procedure. The ASC found a supplier that would employ the same principle for the supplies used in certain common operations. When the kit is opened, everything is in order.

7. **Defects.** Anything that must be done over counts here. Unexpected hospital admissions are an obvious consideration. Also, however, consider outliers such as the patient who stays too long. The ASC marks the clock time whenever the patient stops in any of the five activity areas. Each month, they pull the charts for outliers and analyze the reasons. A Pareto chart indicates the most important area for corrective action. When this disclosed that "waiting for a ride" was a major cause for delayed discharge, the ASC rented beepers for spouses.

In keeping with process thinking under ISO, the surgery center has a single process for patients having surgery with anesthesia. Within that process, five activities take place while the patient is in the building: registration, pre-op, OR, recovery, and discharge. (For this discussion we'll ignore the scheduling and pre-visit activities.)

Each quarter, senior management looks at defined indicators for the surgery process: utilization of the ORs, supply costs, personnel costs, unexpected admissions, and so on. The Lean principles help improve the activities in each area and contribute to the overall success of the ASC. The ISO standards require that the ASC improve its processes of care but does not specify the use of Lean to accomplish that goal.

SIX SIGMA

Six Sigma is another quality tool that many organizations have found useful, particularly for solving problems that extend to multiple disciplines or sections. Originally based on error reduction, the concept has evolved to an orderly team-based approach to solving problems. The actual tools used to solve the problem are left to the team members, but they must follow an orderly process to:

1. **D**efine the problem. Equally important in some cases is to define what is *not* part of the problem. Draw lines around the scope of work to ensure that it is manageable.

2. **M**easure the current state of the problem and establish metrics to demonstrate improvement.

3. **A**ssess the results of metrics and decide on an improvement strategy.

4. Implement the improvements and determine that they did, indeed, solve the problem.

5. Control the process going forward to establish the changes as part of the culture and thus ensure that the improvements will continue.

This process is termed *DMAIC* in the parlance of Six Sigma. Although Six Sigma is not mentioned in the ISO standards, any organization is free to use this technique for the required improvements.

SUMMARY

Many other tools and techniques are useful for improving processes within a healthcare organization. The specific culture within the organization may promote one or more of these, and the ISO standards allow for any or all. ISO requires that you measure what you are doing and demonstrate improvement. The defining characteristic of ISO is that it does not specify any single approach.

6

Clinical Integration as Facilitated by a Quality Management System

The present system of healthcare in the United States is expensive and fragmented. Although the care provided in acute settings is often excellent quality, the overall care provided is not at the same level as that provided in other developed countries.[1] On a positive note, recent legislation as well as economic forces and technological improvements will likely enable providers to share information both in clinic or office-based electronic health record (EHR) systems and in more sophisticated health information exchanges involving multiple provider entities such as hospitals, physicians, nursing homes, wound clinics, and pharmacies.

Clinical integration is a term used to describe alignment among provider entities, usually referring to hospitals and physicians. There are many types of integration, ranging from sharing common EHR platforms in PHO or IPA settings to full employment. It is generally a structured collaboration with a goal of greater quality and efficiency of care delivery. Although the types of integration will dictate the degree to which a QMS is beneficial, this chapter will describe the ways in which a QMS generally facilitates clinical integration. For purposes of discussion, an ISO 9001 QMS will be discussed.

START SIMPLE: ALIGN A FEW KEY DOCUMENTS/PROCESSES

The controlled document system required by the ISO 9001 standard can by employed to monitor and integrate key processes of organizations that are becoming clinically integrated. For example, a physician clinic becoming integrated with a hospital may want to compare the registration processes between the two entities in order to identify potential problems and opportunities to improve efficiency. Mapping the initial registration process within an ISO QMS framework for each organization can reveal a number of issues (see Figure 6.1).

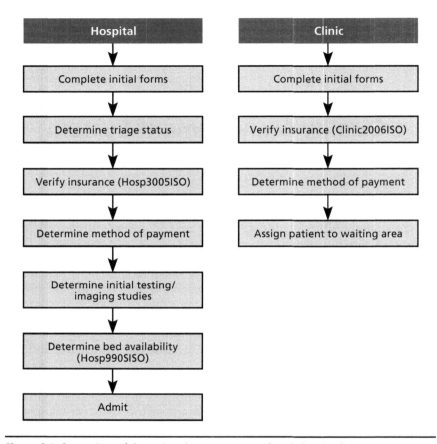

Figure 6.1 Comparison of the registration processes at a hospital and a clinic.

In this example, the process steps are not aligned since the hospital registration is more complex. Although there may be an opportunity to lean the hospital process, it could also be aligned via the controlled document system. In this case, both entities verify insurance and describe it in related documents, so they can easily be compared and mapped against one another. The factor that enables this is the controlled document system of each organization. Although the document systems may not be aligned, the fact that they are in place makes it relatively simple to identify similar processes, protocols, and procedures and to map them against one another. In later iterations of the document systems, a common numbering scheme for the documents may be developed as they become more integrated.

Another example of such integration is provided by experience in a typical surgery center where complaints are received from patients who were asked for insurance information. A patient may respond, "I already gave this to the surgeon's office nurse a week ago!" Listening to these complaints and developing a process to get the information from the surgeon's office can be facilitated if both organizations have a common platform to define, manage, and share information within a QMS framework. In this way, documents can be standardized, defined, numbered, and then tracked so that future changes are recorded in both organizations and improvements are sustained.

OTHER COMPONENTS OF CLINICAL INTEGRATION

Almost every feature of a healthcare organization can be incorporated into a QMS. In fact, the true value of a QMS is that, although it requires that certain features be in place, it also allows the individual organization to add or incorporate any additional features or components that it feels are important. The *what* is required, but the *how* is open to interpretation by each individual organization. Several clinical integration components/ entities are listed in Table 6.1.

Table 6.1 Components of clinical integration related to features of the ISO 9001 QMS.

Clinical Integration Component	ISO 9001 QMS Features				
	Auditing	Corrective/ Preventive Action Plans	Document System	Management Review	Quality Policy, Objectives, Manual
Ambulatory Facilities/Long-term Care Facilities/ Wound Clinics	X	X	X	X	X
Clinical Protocols	X	X	X	X	X
Coding/Billing	X	X	X	X	X
Disease Registries	X		X	X	
EHR/IT	X	X	X	X	X
Performance Measures/PQRS	X		X	X	X
Transitions of Care	X	X	X	X	X
Workflow/Process Mapping	X		X	X	X

In Table 6.1, the clinical integration components listed in the left column are juxtaposed with the key features of an ISO 9001 QMS. In general, almost all key features of a QMS are appropriate and, in fact, helpful to use in both developing and monitoring the work of clinical integration. For example, integrating outpatient facilities with a hospital system is greatly facilitated by an aligned document system, common quality and business objectives, a common corrective and preventive action plan process, system-wide auditing, and a common management review process. Having an aligned QMS in each organization with common quality objectives and a scorecard also enables the development and collection of performance measurements that can be used in each setting and easily incorporated into the QMS. This will be discussed in more detail in Chapter 7.

In response to recent federal legislation, healthcare organizations are incorporating more electronic health record (EHR) and computerized physician order entry (CPOE) systems. The concept of "meaningful use" is important for all organizations to understand and achieve, and other important IT issues relate to data encryption, identity management, firewalls, and protecting personally identifiable information from breaches. In order to deal with these types of regulations and requirements, healthcare organizations must develop risk assessment procedures, audits, and security plans on a system-wide basis. All of these steps can be facilitated by a common QMS platform. Those interested in obtaining a high level of understanding and implementing a formal information security management system can consult the ISO 27000 information security standard.

SPECIFIC FEATURES OF THE ISO 9001 STANDARD RELATED TO CLINICAL INTEGRATION

In a detailed review of the ISO standard (ANSI/ISO/ASQ Q9001-2008), we see that the following clauses and clause requirements seem most appropriate and applicable to the issue of clinical integration:

4. Quality management system
    4.2.1 General documentation requirements
        a. documented statements of a quality policy and quality objectives
        b. a quality manual
        c. documented procedures and records required by the International Standard
        d. documents, including records, determined by the organization to be necessary to ensure the effective planning, operation, and control of its processes

4.2.2 Quality manual
4.2.3 Control of documents
4.2.4 Control of records

5. Management responsibility
   5.4   Planning
   5.6   Management review

6. Resource management
   6.2.2 Competence, training, and awareness

7. Service realization
   7.2.1 Determination of requirements related to the service
   7.4   Purchasing
   7.5   Service provision

8. Measurement, analysis, and improvement
   8.2.1 Customer satisfaction
   8.2.2 Internal audit
   8.4   Analysis of data
   8.5   Improvement
   8.5.1 Continual improvement
   8.5.2 Corrective action
   8.5.3 Preventive action

The details of each of these clauses and sections may be viewed online at www.iso.org. It is important to note that, in general, these clauses describe the *what* more than the *how* for any given requirement. For example, internal audits (the *what*) are required by the standard, but the scope, criteria, frequency and methods (the *how*) are up to the organization and must simply be defined and followed. Each organization has the freedom to design its QMS in a way that is reasonable, fits its workflow issues, and works within the context of the organization. An organization developing a clinical integration strategy may thus incorporate into its QMS whatever policies, protocols, processes, or other ideas desired by the organization to achieve its particular goals and strategic objectives.

BARRIERS TO CLINICAL INTEGRATION

There are many barriers to clinical integration, including cultural, geographic, and economic/payment issues. The concept of clinical integration has sparked the interest of most healthcare systems over the last few years, and many successful models will no doubt be established. As experience in clinical integration increases, many of the barriers will be overcome, although in the final analysis, success will depend upon the ability of the participants to establish rules and organizational structures that ensure success. Having a QMS in place provides the structure necessary to serve as a platform for clinical integration, and it is likely to become one of the models used by successful healthcare organizations.

References

1. Organization for Economic Cooperation and Development, "Health Expenditure," 220–221. *OECD Factbook*, 2009.

7

Using ISO 9001 as the Foundation for a Performance Improvement System

Many aspects of a QMS provide the foundation for a performance improvement system. The idea of a performance improvement system is to first develop meaningful measures in areas of interest such as clinical outcomes, cost, patient safety, efficiency, and patient satisfaction. Assessments are then used to provide feedback on how the measures are proceeding toward established goals and objectives. Success requires clear and understandable measures, well-defined goals, teamwork, and appropriate processes and structures. Throwing in a little dose of systems thinking doesn't hurt, either. This process is enabled by an integrated framework such as that of a QMS. One might think of the QMS as providing ongoing assessments using audits and quality surveillance via the management review and corrective and preventive action programs.

THE ISO 9001 STANDARD AND PERFORMANCE IMPROVEMENT

A review of the ANSI/ISO/ASQ Q9001–2008 standard provides an overview of how an organization might use ISO 9001 as the foundation for a performance improvement system. Some of the specific clauses and subclauses of the standard that address performance improvement are outlined below with comments that describe the particular application.

4.2.2   Quality manual

- The quality manual is the basic document used to describe how the organization does business and manages its processes. Descriptions of the performance improvement program can be easily incorporated into the quality manual, and suggested clauses/subclauses that may be appropriate follow.

5.3   Quality policy

- A description of the performance improvement system may be included in the quality policy.

5.4.1 Quality objectives

- Objectives are described in this subclause. It may be useful to include a reference to the performance improvement system. Also, the organization's unique quality objectives are listed here. For example, an organization that plans to undertake a formal risk assessment every two years would state this under its quality objectives. Thus it will be held accountable for doing the assessment by the ISO audit system.

5.6   Management review

- All components of the ISO 9001 QMS are evaluated by management review. Specifically subclause 5.6.2, review input, is used to gather information from sources such as audits, customer feedback, and corrective and preventive actions. Furthermore, subclause 5.6.3 states that review output is used to monitor decisions and improvements planned and is implemented through the management review process. Both of these processes fit nicely within the context of a performance improvement system. Including creation of a performance improvement system within the QMS ensures that information is gathered and decisions are implemented, since there is oversight from both the audit system and management review.

7.2.1 Determination of requirements related to the service

7.2.2 Review of requirements related to the service

- These are key aspects of any performance improvement system and represent basic methods for determining customer requirements and the organization's ability to meet those requirements.

8.2   Monitoring and measurement

8.2.1 Customer satisfaction

8.2.2 Internal audit

8.2.3 Monitoring and measurement of processes

8.2.4 Monitoring and measurement of services

8.3   Control of nonconforming service

- Specific subclauses address the ideas of monitoring and measuring customer satisfaction, processes, and service delivery using the ISO internal audit system.

8.4   Analysis of data

- Data analysis is an important aspect of any performance improvement system.

8.5   Improvement

8.5.1   Continual improvement

8.5.2   Corrective action

8.5.3   Preventive action

- The ISO 9001 standard requires the organization to continually improve the effectiveness of its QMS using all of its components, and specifically by making use of its corrective and preventive action procedures.

USING AN ISO QMS TO SUPPORT DATA COLLECTION FOR THE PHYSICIAN QUALITY REPORTING SYSTEM (PQRS)

The Centers for Medicare and Medicaid Services (CMS) established the PQRS program to collect quality metrics from physicians in different specialties, who are then rewarded for achieving target rates of reporting various disease conditions. This program was initially termed the Physician Quality Reporting Initiative (PQRI); it was changed to the Physician Quality Reporting System (PQRS) in 2011. It is a good example of the way in which an ISO 9001 QMS controlled document system may be used to track metrics for a given specialty or group of specialties. Figure 7.1 represents the peri-operative PQRI measures required for surgeons in 2010. It is in the standard document format used at Physicians' Clinic of Iowa with a clear title, purpose, list of definitions/acronyms, procedural description, associated records, and revision history.

Document Title	Number	Rev.
2010 PQRI Peri-operative Care Measures Group	6103PCI	1.0

Purpose (outline the intent or objective of the document)
A list of the 2010 Peri-operative Care Measures Group.
Definitions and Acronyms (provide clear understanding for words and abbreviations that may be ambiguous)
PQRI = Physician Quality Reporting Initiative
Procedure/Flowchart (describe the steps in which work objectives are achieved; include statements, to the extent necessary, that explain the *why, what, when, where, who,* and *how*)

Measure #20: Peri-operative Care: Timing of Antibiotic Prophylaxis – Ordering Physician
- Patients 18 years and older who have an order for prophylactic antibiotic to be given within one hour (if fluroquinolone or vancomycin, two hours) prior to the surgical incision (or start of procedure when no incision is required).
- **CPT 4047F** – Written, verbal, or standing order for prophylactic antibiotic.
OR
- **CPT 4048F** – Documentation that prophylactic antibiotic has been given
  Modifier 1P – Order for prophylactic antibiotic *not given* for medical reasons.
  Modifier 8P – Order *not given,* reason *not specified.*

Measure #21: Peri-operative Care: Selection of Prophylactic Antibiotic, First or Second Generation
Cephalosporin
- Patients 18 years and older who have an order for cefazolin or cefuroxine for antimicrobial prophylaxis.
  CPT 4041F – Written, verbal, or standing order for cefazolin or cefuroxine.
  Modifier 1P – Cefazolin or Cefuroxine *not ordered* for medical reasons.
  Modifier 8P – Cefazolin or Cefuroxine *not ordered,* reason *not specified.*

Measure #22: Peri-operative Care: Discontinuation of Prophylactic Antibiotic
- Patients 18 years and older who received a prophylactic antibiotic have an order to discontinue the prophylactic antibiotic within 24 hours of the surgical end time.
- **CPT 4049F** – Written, verbal, or standing order for discontinuation of antibiotic within 24 hours.
  and
  CPT 4046F – Documentation that prophylactic antibiotics were given within 4 hours prior to surgical incision
OR
- **Modifier 1P** – Prophylactic antibiotic *not discontinued* for medical reasons.
  and
  CPT 4046F – Documentation that prophylactic antibiotics were given within 4 hours prior to surgical incision
OR
- **Modifier 8P** – Prophylactic antibiotic *not discontinued,* reason *not specified.*
  and
  CPT 4046F – Documentation that prophylactic antibiotics were given within 4 hours prior to surgical incision

Figure 7.1 PCI document of 2010 PQRI peri-operative measures.   *(Continued)*

(Continued)

Measure #23: Venous Thromboembolism (VTE) Prophylaxis (When Indicated in All Patients)

- Patients 18 years and older undergoing procedures for which VTE prophylaxis is indicated in all patients, who had an order for Low Molecular Weight Heparin, Low-Dose Unfractionated Heparin, adjusted-dose warfarin, fondaparinux, or mechanical prophylaxis to be given within 24 hours prior to incision time or within 24 hours after surgery end time.
  CPT 4044F – Written, verbal, or standing order for VTE prophylaxis.
  Modifier 1P – VTE *not ordered* for medical reasons.
  Modifier 8P – VTE prophylaxis *not ordered,* reason *not specified.*

Records: (Results or evidence of work performed.)
Medical record file.

Revision	Description of Change	Approval	Date
1	Initial draft	F. Jones	3-12-10

Figure 7.1 PCI document of 2010 PQRI peri-operative measures.

The advantage in using an ISO documentation system is that the documents are clear and available and can be easily updated. The system provides a framework for determining operational definitions and for reporting criteria. This is valuable in developing a performance improvement system for any healthcare organization.

THE ISO QMS AND THE BALANCED SCORECARD/STRATEGY MAP

Many healthcare organizations lack an effective management system that can integrate and align the clinical and non-clinical processes and activities, facilitating maximal performance and value for the organization. In healthcare, most processes are managed independently instead of systematically, so platforms that provide integration are of value. The ISO 9001 QMS represents a framework that can be used to both collect data and to present data in an understandable way utilizing tools such as a balanced scorecard. The concept of the balanced scorecard was developed by Kaplan and Norton in 1992. Although newer versions have been described, it remains anchored by these four main perspectives: learning and growth, internal, customer, and financial.[1] These can be represented using a strategy map such as that shown in Figure 7.2 for our fictitious Medical Group of the Upper Midwest.

Medical Group of the Upper Midwest

Vision: The Medical Group of the Upper Midwest provides coordinated, value-driven care of the highest quality while being the patient's advocate and employing sound business practices.

Financial Perspective:

Value

Cost Effectiveness

Increased Market Share & Revenue

Integration

New Providers   Ancillary Services

Value Proposition: Deliver coordinated, value-driven medical care of the highest quality

Customer Perspective:

Patients	Referring Physicians	Payers/ Employers	Shareholders	Outcome Measures	Employees
Patient advocacy	Timely correspondence	Strong relationships	Physician quality	High-value internal processes	Staff quality
Excellent service	Leading-edge expertise	Innovative programs	Leadership strength	Physician quality	High satisfaction
Educational programs	Educational programs Outreach activities			Reporting initiative	

Internal Perspective:

Operations Management		Customer Management	Innovation	Regulatory and Social
Healthcare Processes	**Support Processes**	Relationship with partners	Surgical procedures	Risk management
Physician care	Accounting/ revenue	Marketing – charitable foundation	Quality systems	Compliance
Clinical staff care	Human resources			Credentialing
Patient family education	Contracting			Community health promotion
	Management review			
	Purchasing			

Figure 7.2 Medical Group of the Upper Midwest strategy map.   *(Continued)*

(Continued)

Learning and Growth Perspective:

Human Capital	Information Capital	Organizational Capital
Continuous educational programs	Infrastructure	Governance
Employee assistance programs	EHR	Management
Entertainment events	Software programs	Quality management systems – ISO 9001
	Data collection committee	Balanced scorecards
	Satisfaction surveys	Strategy maps
	Employees	
	Patients	
	Referring physicians	
	Shareholders	
	Physician performance metrics	

Figure 7.2 Medical Group of the Upper Midwest strategy map.

In this example, each perspective is clearly outlined and one can understand the components within the organization that support the perspective. Thus, it is clear that for this organization it is important to provide patients with advocacy, excellent service, and educational programs (customer perspective) supported by an infrastructure that includes an EHR, data collection, patient satisfaction surveys, and measurement of physician performance metrics (learning and growth perspective). These services and processes can be incorporated into the ISO QMS, which then ensures that they are implemented and monitored by the ISO system of auditing, corrective/preventive action plans, and management review. In a simple example, providing excellent customer service is achieved by determination and review of requirements related to the service (what the customer wants/needs; 7.2.1, 7.2.2) and is monitored via customer satisfaction surveys and analysis of data (8.2.1, 8.4). Many healthcare organizations utilize conventional balanced score-cards constructed as tables, but the strategy map is of interest for the reasons mentioned above.

PATIENT SAFETY AND REPORTING

An ISO QMS may also be utilized as the foundation of a patient safety and reporting system. Reporting systems are becoming increasingly important with the advent of patient safety organizations (PSOs) and the numerous articles reporting adverse events. CMS currently refuses to pay for certain hospital-acquired conditions such as foreign objects retained after surgery, stage III and IV pressure ulcers, and catheter-associated urinary tract infections. In fact, CMS is considering expanding this list of "never events"; the policy will have a major effect on hospitals not in compliance. Among the ideas for decreasing these adverse events are the following:

- Broaden and clarify the definitions of adverse events.

- Create clear goals for improvement.

- Establish incentives for improvement and disincentives for errors.

Several steps may be undertaken within the ISO QMS to accomplish the task of increasing reporting:

- Utilize the document system to clearly explain each error with a formal operational definition.

- Develop a flow chart to outline the steps for reporting an error, including who reports, how to report (paper, electronic system), and other steps.

- Write a reporting document that is used to record important information regarding the event, such as reporter identity, location, environmental factors, other factors, and special circumstances. This document may be paper or electronic.

With the reporting system in place, the documents become available and the work effort and documents are incorporated into the quality manual. As in the other examples, oversight is provided by internal auditing, management review, and corrective and preventive action plans.

RISK ASSESSMENT

Similar to the ways in which the QMS might be used for patient safety reporting, it also lends itself to developing a risk assessment program. The risk assessment program may be easily incorporated into the framework of an ISO QMS using the clauses and subclauses mentioned earlier. One example of such a risk assessment program is provided by the aforementioned fictitious Medical Group of the Upper Midwest, which undertook a risk assessment last year and was provided the following report by its insurance carrier (Table 7.1).

Table 7.1 Risk assessment of Medical Group of the Upper Midwest.

Observation	Recommendations
Medical record entries were inconsistently dated.	All entries in the medical record, including scanned documents, must be dated with month, day, and year of the interaction or entry.
Reviewed medical records contained abnormal lab or test results with no documented communication of these results to the patient.	The organization must develop a system to verify that all patients with normal and/or abnormal lab results or tests are notified in a timely manner. As a practical matter, the physician should review all results as soon as available rather than waiting for the patient's return appointment. Always document all correspondence related to the results.
Prescription pads are not secure.	Prescription pads should be stored in a locked drawer or other safe location not visible to the patient.
Incomplete documentation of the medication prescribed.	Any medication prescribed by a provider should include date, drug name, dosage, frequency, and number of refills followed by the provider's signature. Any drug instructions and precautions provided to the patient should be documented.
No written telephone triage protocols.	Physicians should write telephone triage protocols for office and after-hour calls. The protocols should address frequently asked questions, general guidelines to determine whether an office visit or other action is necessary, and the types of complaints that require immediate attention.
After-hour phone calls are inconsistently documented.	All patient phone calls should be documented and should include: • The date and time of the call • Subjective information provided by the patient or family member • Medical advice given • If applicable, Rx phoned to pharmacy • Authentication of staff taking the call • If handled by staff and not a provider, evidence that the physician provided direction
Telephone calls do not show evidence of physician's involvement.	Physicians must verify communication where medical advice was given. Failure to verify may give the appearance that the clinical staff is functioning outside their scope of practice.
Tracking systems are inconsistently applied by providers.	Tracking of patient results and missed/cancelled appointments is a critical function. When test results are lost and/or missed appointments are not tracked, the appropriate follow-up is not likely to be implemented.

The decision to do a risk assessment can be documented by placing a statement into the quality manual. Clause 5, Management Responsibility, contains subclause 5.4, Planning; an organizational statement may be added under this subclause stating, for example, that the organization will perform a risk assessment every two years. As in other examples, the QMS assures that the assessment will be conducted, audited, and discussed at the management review. Specific observations and recommendations such as those listed above can then be incorporated into the QMS using the systems approach described in this book.

MEANINGFUL USE

In order for hospitals and eligible providers to receive payments from CMS for using EHR systems, they must demonstrate "meaningful use" of their electronic systems. Meaningful use criteria have been described by CMS for both hospitals and eligible providers, and the QMS may be utilized to keep track of and manage some of the requirements of the criteria. The American Recovery and Reinvestment Act of 2009 specifies three main components of meaningful use:

- The use of a certified EHR for a meaningful purpose, such as e-prescribing.

- The use of certified EHR technology for electronic exchange of health information to improve quality of healthcare.

- The use of certified EHR technology to submit clinical quality and other measures.

The core objectives hospitals must meet are listed below:

1. Perform computerized physician order entry (CPOE)

2. Perform drug–drug and drug–allergy interaction checks

3. Record demographics

4. Implement one clinical decision support rule

5. Maintain an up-to-date problem list of current and active diagnoses

6. Maintain an active medication list

7. Maintain an active medication allergy list

8. Record and chart changes in vital signs

9. Record smoking status for patients 13 years and older

10. Report hospital clinical quality measures to CMS or a state authority

11. Provide patients with an electronic copy of their health information upon request

12. Provide patients with an electronic copy of their discharge instructions at the time of discharge upon request

13. Exchange key clinical information among providers of care and patient-authorized entities electronically

14. Protect electronic health information

In addition to this core set of objectives, there is a set of menu-driven objectives, five of which must be chosen by each hospital. These can be reviewed at: www.cms.gov/EHRIncentivePrograms/30_Meaningful_Use Hospitals must also collect the following clinical quality measures:

1. Emergency Department Throughput – admitted patients – Median time from ED arrival to ED departure for admitted patients

2. Emergency Department Throughput – admitted patients – Admission decision time to ED departure time for admitted patients

3. Ischemic stroke – Discharge on anti-thrombotics

4. Ischemic stroke – Anticoagulation for atrial fibrillation/flutter

5. Ischemic stroke – Thrombolytic therapy for patients arriving within 2 hours of symptom onset

6. Ischemic or hemorrhagic stroke – Antithrombotic therapy by day 2

7. Ischemic stroke – Discharge on statins

8. Ischemic or hemorrhagic stroke – Stroke education

9. Ischemic or hemorrhagic stroke – Rehabilitation assessment

10. Venous thromboembolism (VTE) prophylaxis within 24 hours of arrival

11. Intensive Care Unit VTE prophylaxis

12. Anticoagulation overlap therapy

13. Platelet monitoring on unfractionated heparin

14. VTE discharge instructions

15. Incidence of potentially preventable VTE

The core objectives, menu set objectives, and clinical quality measures all require utilization of a certified electronic health record system as described in the CMS guidelines. The ability of an organization to meet these requirements is facilitated by a QMS for three specific reasons:

1. Operational definitions can be clearly stated in the appropriate documents sent to specific areas/departments of interest such as the ED, intensive care unit, and neurology floor for clinical quality measures 3 through 9. Documents can be maintained, updated, and deleted as appropriate.

2. Documents describing collection processes and meaningful use requirements can be incorporated into flowcharts and process maps as they are developed, thereby facilitating understanding and ensuring that the requirements are met and that the data are collected.

3. Placing the meaningful use collection processes into the CMS framework ensures that the system will be audited and reviewed.

References

1. R. Kaplan and D. Norton, "The Balanced Scorecard—Measures that Drive Performance," *Harvard Business Review* (January/February 1992): 92–100.

8

Experience with ISO 9001 in a Multi-specialty Clinic

Physicians' Clinic of Iowa (PCI) is a 55-physician clinic in Cedar Rapids with physician specialties including cardiac surgery, otolaryngology, general surgery, neurology, oncology, orthopedic surgery, podiatry, rheumatology, thoracic surgery, urology, and vascular surgery. PCI employs 275 staff at five locations. PCI physicians manage approximately 150,000 E & M encounters and perform more than 60,000 surgical procedures annually. PCI leadership elected to pursue ISO 9001 registration in the spring of 2001 and the clinic was formally registered to ISO 9001:2000 in November 2003. This chapter describes the concept and requirements of the ISO 9001 quality management system, the PCI implementation experience and costs, and the results achieved during the first year of certification.

ISO 9001 BACKGROUND AND REQUIREMENTS

As discussed in Chapter 2, the International Organization for Standardization (ISO) was founded in Geneva in 1947 to provide standardization of technical specifications for products traded in the international marketplace.[1] Over the years the concept of standardization has evolved from that of specific technical specifications to a broader concept of generic QMS standards. An organization becoming certified to ISO 9001 is essentially establishing a QMS that provides for work performance consistency, stresses the process approach, defines goals and objectives for quality, provides benchmarks to measure improvements, and requires identification and evaluation of causes of poor performance. An organization seeking ISO registration is required to describe and implement a QMS according to the requirements of the American National Standard for quality management systems.[2] This involves writing a quality policy, quality manual, and quality objectives and then utilizing the process approach to address the other requirements of the standard.

ISO 9000 is the family of standards; an entity is registered to ISO 9001:2008. ISO 9001 requirements are based on the following eight quality management principles:

- Customer focus
- Leadership
- Involvement of people
- Process approach
- Systems approach to management
- Continual improvement
- Factual approach to decision making
- Mutually beneficial supplier relationships

The principles are imbedded within the eight clauses of ISO 9001:2008 that comprise the quality manual for an organization, and together they describe the QMS. A QMS may thus be described as a set of processes that provide direction and control of an organization's quality.

ISO IMPLEMENTATION AND COSTS

The experience at PCI was carefully documented over the two and a half years during which it worked to become registered. During the first year, PCI leadership identified a local consultant experienced in ISO certification for businesses, established an ISO steering committee, conducted several ISO kick-off meetings and training sessions for employees, and visited local businesses that offered tours of their facilities and shared information about their ISO QMSs. A quality policy, quality objectives, and a quality manual were written and circulated to employees. Employee support for the project was obtained by actively engaging them in designing the QMS. In many cases employees were asked to describe their job responsibilities as ISO documents were written. This employee involvement was key, as they learned that the QMS was not a threat to them but rather a supporting framework that would allow them to improve their clinical and business processes.

The first milestone was the development of a controlled document system using an alphanumeric numbering system. All policies and procedures were reviewed, revised, and put into a common document format. PCI had more than 400 policies and procedures in place when the process began; it reduced the number of documents to 375 by the time of registration, including the addition of new policies and procedures required by ISO. Standardizing medical records among different departments and sites of care was a major work effort, but it was important in understanding the value of having a common document system within the organization. It also became apparent that the HIPAA requirements for healthcare providers were much easier to implement with an ISO QMS in place.

During the second year, PCI selected TUV America as its registrar and developed process maps for the overall clinical patient flow process, medical patient care process, and surgical patient care process. It also conducted a quality training retreat for all interested employees. The second milestone was the internal auditor training sessions provided by the consultant. These sessions involved employees from each office and were valuable in teaching auditing principles and in clarifying the value of auditing for monitoring and improving the QMS. PCI also instituted management review meetings, which are held every six months and are designed to oversee the QMS, monitor issues, provide follow-up to corrective and preventive actions, and measure process improvement. A physician quality council was established with representatives from each specialty department; it serves as a conduit to keep physicians informed within respective departments. Furthermore, PCI established a data collection committee with quality improvement representatives from each of two community hospitals for the purpose of obtaining data for metrics residing in the hospital databases. The second year also marked the establishment of the PCI quality newsletter, *PCIntouch*. The newsletter is written monthly and focuses on both HIPAA and ISO 9001 issues.

During the final six months of ISO certification, the PCI chief medical officer wrote a series of physician newsletters focusing on basic ISO concepts and employees participated in a practice audit conducted by the consultant and several local quality managers within the industry. PCI underwent a pre-assessment audit conducted by TUV two months prior to its formal registration audit. It became registered to ISO 9001:2000 on November 10, 2003. PCI is the largest medical group in the United States to have attained ISO certification.

Documentation of PCI's ISO experience involved maintaining records of all meetings and attendees. Using this information, the soft costs of implementing the ISO QMS based on 142 meetings from March 1 through September 3 were calculated. A total of 2,345 hours of FTE time was calculated at the hourly rate for each attendee, for a soft cost total of $81,895 (0.5% of the total payroll). The hard costs included consultant costs, pre-audit by the registrar, and formal audit by the registrar, totaling $26,547. Total costs were thus calculated:

- Total costs to date of certification. . . . . $ 108,443
- Cost per physician . . . . $ 2,169
- Cost per physician per year (over 2.5 yr.). . . . . $ 868

Although the soft costs calculation is accurate, the meetings often involved PCI business dealing with clinical issues not associated with

ISO implementation. It is estimated that half of the soft costs involved time that would have been required from employees without the ISO QMS. Calculation of costs per physician per year, then, equates to $540 rather than $868.

COST SAVINGS ATTRIBUTED TO ISO IMPLEMENTATION

The major cost savings resulting from implementation of the ISO 9001 QMS are due to improvements in process management. The process approach is a fundamental principle of ISO 9001, and the clinical and support processes at PCI were defined and analyzed early during ISO implementation. This effort involved an evaluation of its business processes and resulted in a reduction of days in accounts receivable from 66 to 46, with a one-time $72,500 of additional income (Figure 8.1).

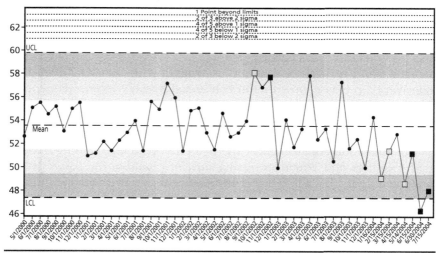

Physician's Clinic of Iowa, PC
Days in AR
Total
Individuals
Temporary: UCL=59.72, Mean=53.50, LCL=47.29 (mR=2)

Figure 8.1 PCI days in accounts receivable.

A second area of increased income resulting from the process approach involved an analysis of actual reimbursement against payer-contracted reimbursement. The process approach led to a careful analysis of these rates, and as a result $100,000 in underpayments on contracted rates during the first year was identified.

An important aspect of ISO 9001 is the concept of standardizing purchased products and services. ISO 9001 includes Clause 7 Service Realization, with subclause 7.4 describing the purchasing process. The requirement is that organizations have methods to assure that purchased products and services conform to requirements, that suppliers are evaluated on their ability to supply products and services in accordance with the requirements, and that specific criteria are defined for the selection and evaluation of suppliers. PCI enlisted the help of a local industry expert in Lean systems and convened a one-day *kaizen* event to evaluate the system and identify changes to be implemented within PCI. The process initially involved value stream mapping of the current purchasing process shown in Figure 8.2. The next step was to develop a vision for the ideal purchasing process. The ideal state would involve economies of scale, be efficient, and include an automated purchasing order system; it would be simple, consistent, low cost, high quality, and easily monitored. Specific objectives for developing an ideal purchasing process were identified:

- Create a standardized process
- Create a trackable process
- Create guidelines
- Identify preferred vendors
- Establish effective avenues to share information

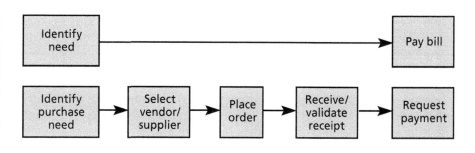

Figure 8.2 PCI purchasing process.

Early results for PCI's redesigned purchasing process included a 42% savings in shredding costs. Additional savings in cleaning, snow removal, garage disposal, recycling, liability insurance, and medical waste were also realized during 2005.

Another area of cost savings involved restructuring the workers' compensation program. PCI leadership initially reviewed the process and initiated an in-house nuisance claims fund of several thousand dollars to address low-level claims in a timely manner. This was combined with education of the occupational medicine staff, department directors, and employees. An "alternate duty program" was initiated for employees in areas at risk of injury, such as radiology techs involved with lifting patients on a daily basis. An ergonomic review was conducted in clerical and clinical areas to identify potential problems and employees at risk.

Several procedures were redesigned within the workers' compensation program. Internal reporting for potential claims was changed to ensure notification of both the director of human resources and the appropriate department director. PCI established on-going risk management assessments in partnership with its insurance carrier and the human resources department. The major change relating to the claims process itself was to require external rather than internal clinical evaluation for the employee making the claim. This resulted in fewer nuisance claims.

As a result of using the process approach within the ISO 9001 QMS, PCI demonstrated a significant reduction in claims for workers' compensation between 2001 and 2004 (Figure 8.3). Because of this improvement, the insurance carrier agreed to reduce the annual premium for 2004 workers' compensation insurance by $45,000. Figure 8.3 depicts the frequency of workers' compensation claims and the mod rate. Mod rate is the experience modification factor that compares actual loss with expected loss over a period of time. If losses are lower than expected for the industry, the mod rate should be less than 1.0; if losses are higher than expected, the mod will be greater than 1.0. The industry standard is 1.0, which represents the average amount of claims in a given industry.

The cost savings outlined above totaled approximately $220,000 and were identified during the initial twelve months of ISO implementation. Some of the cost savings would have been achieved without the ISO QMS, although the process was clearly improved and more efficient because of the QMS and the concepts derived from ISO 9001. Even half of the cost savings, $110,000, would have paid for the total cost of implementing the QMS, $108,443, with soft costs included.

COMMUNITY BENEFITS OF ISO IMPLEMENTATION

During the ISO implementation process a PCI quality council was established to help develop the clinical quality program and identify key quality indicators. The council consisted of one physician from each specialty at PCI, and each physician was asked to determine metrics of value for his/her specialty. The council identified 55 indicators among 10

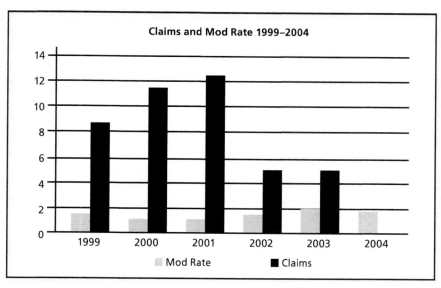

Figure 8.3 PCI workers' compensation claims.

specialties. In evaluating the indicators, it became apparent that operational definitions were unclear, the process of data collection was difficult, and PCI was unable to collect indicators without the help of the two community hospitals. Therefore, a second quality committee, the data collection committee, was established with quality improvement (QI) representatives of both hospitals and PCI. The committee reviewed the requested data and decided to focus on what the hospitals had already collected. Many physicians had an interest in antibiotic administration, and this interest coincided with a project of the Iowa Foundation for Medical Care (IFMC), the quality improvement organization in Iowa. The committee chose to work together on the national Surgical Infection Prevention (SIP) project sponsored by Medicare, with the idea that the project would be a combined effort of all three entities. The SIP indicators were:

- Antibiotic administration within one hour of the surgical incision
- Use of appropriate antibiotic
- Discontinuation of antibiotic use within 24 hours

Mercy Medical Center and St. Luke's Hospital agreed to collect the three SIP indicators while PCI would provide the rate of surgical-site wound infection after discharge from the hospitals. This ability to track wound infections in a clinical setting improved the overall understanding of community infection rates; it was implemented by developing an ISO document for tracking wound infections that was maintained by the nurses in each PCI surgical office. Initial results of the collaborative effort for orthopedic patients during 2003 are shown in Figure 8.4. A joint presentation by representatives of PCI and both hospitals was given at the annual IFMC quality conference in November of 2003. Results of the SIP indicator project were presented and the group described the concept of using an ISO QMS to serve as a framework of cooperation within a community of diverse and competing providers.

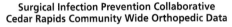

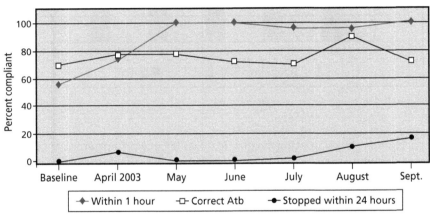

Figure 8.4 SIP orthopedic indicators in Cedar Rapids.

ADDITIONAL CLINIC BENEFITS OF ISO IMPLEMENTATION

As noted above, utilization of the process management approach was the key to implementing the ISO QMS and improving both clinical and support processes at PCI. The process approach was used in initially designing the medical and surgical patient care process maps that were integrated into the ISO system during the first six months. These maps were helpful in understanding the process steps as the care processes were evaluated, improved, and incorporated into the ISO framework. Figure 8.5 illustrates several initial steps in the PCI clinical patient flow process. The key point in this illustration is that the process map is linked to ISO documents using the standard PCI document system developed within the ISO QMS (ISO documents are underlined and numbered to the right). This method facilitates access to written policies and procedures related to and supporting the process map.

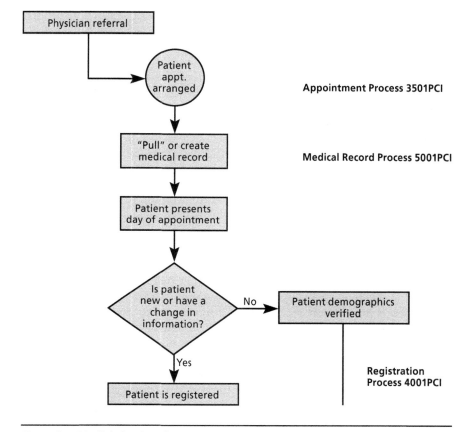

Figure 8.5 PCI clinical patient flow process.

The process approach was also used in developing a balanced scorecard and strategy map for the organization. These documents, described in Chapter 8, were written as a result of the strategic planning process undertaken at PCI biannually. Although the balanced scorecard and strategy maps are not an ISO requirement, they clearly support the ISO management principles outlined above and complement the management review activities required by the ISO 9001 QMS.

The process approach was also used to develop a payer matrix for evaluating payments and contract language on proposed insurance contracts. Through the purchasing process discussed above, a request for proposal (RFP) process was developed and incorporated into the ISO QMS as a methodology to use in obtaining information from vendors. PCI has also used the RFP process to evaluate electronic medical record systems by querying vendors and standardizing categories of comparisons.

The auditing experience at PCI has been positive for both internal and external auditing, which are ISO requirements. PCI has developed an internal auditing program based on training PCI employees, which has been well received and supported by PCI employees. Internal audits are conducted every three to six months and focus on selected areas based on previous audits and findings of non-conformance. The external registrar audit is required annually.

Another aspect of the ISO QMS is the corrective and preventive action procedures required by ISO 9001. This system requirement ensures that any problems identified within the clinic setting receive an adequate and timely follow-up. PCI has incorporated patient comments considered to be of significance into the corrective action plan system as well; the documents are audited and oversight is maintained through the management review process.

SUMMARY

The experience of introducing an ISO 9001 QMS at Physicians' Clinic of Iowa has been very positive. PCI has demonstrated that an ISO QMS provides a framework for quality improvement and for monitoring clinical and business processes. The QMS can be utilized to efficiently implement additional regulatory requirements such as HIPAA, and may serve as a framework to support community healthcare activities as described in Chapter 11. Establishing an ISO QMS requires time and work effort on the part of both employees and management. Although initially planned to be completed within a year, the work took more than two years. Despite this, there was ample time to accomplish the task; in fact, the slower approach made the employees more involved in the process and resulted in a better buy-in. Committed leadership was essential and process management was the most important learning objective gained during the implementation process.

References

1. J. West, C. A. Cianfrani, and J. J. Tsiakals, "Standards outlook quality management principles: foundation of ISO 9000:2000 family," *Quality Progress* 33: 113–116, Feb. 2000.

2. American National Standards Institute, "Quality Management Systems— Requirements," American National Standard (ANSI/ISO/ASQ, Q9001-2000). Washington, D.C., 2000.

9

ISO 9001 at the State Department

THE SETTING

The State Department provides primary care for about 50,000 government employees and their families through embassy health units in almost every country in the world. This network is managed from a central office in Washington, D.C. that also handles global health issues for the State Department as a whole. Other functions for the D.C. office include:

1. **Finance.** Not only budget and finance for the D.C. office, but also funding for evacuation of ill patients from overseas and paying claims for healthcare expenses not covered by insurance.

2. **Purchasing.** Obtaining supplies for the 200-person D.C. headquarters plus setting up mechanisms for local health units to purchase drugs and supplies overseas.

3. **Emergency Preparedness.** Assessing threats to State Department personnel both domestically and overseas. Planning for emergencies such as swine flu and anthrax.

4. **Human Resources.** Hiring for the D.C. office and professional staff for our health units overseas.

5. **Exam Clinic.** Performing physical exams for new employees, retiring employees, and current employees rotating to a new assignment overseas, about 20,000 visits/year.

6. **Laboratory.** Supporting the exam clinic and performing some tests for overseas health units (for example, parasitology).

7. **Clearances.** Evaluating health needs of personnel relative to facilities available overseas.

8. **Quality Improvement (QI).** Performing medical staff functions (credentialing, licensing) and addressing privacy issues and HIPAA compliance. The director of QI serves as the management representative for ISO 9001.

THE BEGINNING

In the fall of 2005, Dr. Larry Brown, then Medical Director at the State Department, decided to adopt ISO 9001 as a management system for the Office of Medical Services (MED). This decision was driven by the realization that the system had grown considerably, and that we were no longer able to manage from the back of an envelope. Some system was needed to keep track of policies and provide them where needed. We realized that we were solving the same problems and making the same mistakes multiple times, because there was no central source for a new policy after the solution had been established. Many sections in MED didn't believe they had customers, and there was no system for establishing customer needs or assessing how well we were meeting those needs. Some processes were slow, but no one knew exactly how slow or whether things were getting better or worse. In other words, we lacked metrics.

For these and myriad other reasons, some type of system was needed. Through a series of meetings, consultations, discussions, and review of documents, we looked seriously at three management systems:

1. The Baldrige Criteria for Performance Excellence. There was some experience with the Baldrige award in MED, and the criteria were understandable. However, the focus of the Baldrige award was "excellence" and we were a long way from that point. Although some parts could be used here and there, the overall system did not seem to provide the comprehensive management system we were looking for.

2. The Joint Commission (TJC). Here again, there was some experience in MED with TJC. We had even had a survey by TJC several years prior. But there were several problems: The standards were fairly prescriptive and didn't fit our global healthcare system well. Even the TJC had a hard time deciding which of their standards to use for their survey. In the end, we decided it was not a good fit.

3. ISO 9001:2000. This was not a slam-dunk. The language was foreign to healthcare—even to English. What's "product realization" anyway? The single factor that turned the trick was the high-level, generic aspect of the standards. We could write our own requirements. The standards told us what areas we needed to address, but the details could be fitted to our unique needs. The other attractive aspect to ISO 9001 was the requirement for outside auditors. Registration must be renewed every three years, and this required periodic outside review. Although the concept of outside auditors is common in healthcare, it was a new idea in the State Department. But at last, we were off and running.

THE DECISION

Dr. Brown sent a memo to the world announcing his decision and allocated about $170,000 for the project. Most of the money was spent for training, and most of the training was Lead Auditor courses. At that time, these were five-day courses—a serious time commitment for our employees. Currently, these courses have been condensed to three days. We also trained internal auditors and held shorter classes on implementation of ISO. The top managers went to a half-day overview class.

Training is good, unless students don't want to learn. We had a few students who were sent to class by their supervisor but who had no real interest in the material. Not only was this a waste of money; these students did not participate in class and impeded the learning of others.

Our scope was limited to the Washington, D.C. office, with the intent of expanding globally in the future, and our training was broadly dispersed throughout the organization, both vertically and horizontally. We trained employees at every level and in every section. Two of the ten senior managers took the Lead Auditor course.

We have money in our current budget to provide in-house training every year for four to eight employees. The intent is to provide a continuous flow of current expert knowledge into the organization to balance fading memories and employee attrition.

The other big budget item was an outside consultant. He provided invaluable assistance in many ways, both large and small, and it's hard to imagine accomplishing this without such assistance.

Another advantage we had was a dedicated QI section of two and a half employees. During this time we also hired a part-time student to help with the clerical functions, so the two full-time employees could focus on establishing the ISO system. Both of these individuals took the Lead Auditor course, so we had maximum expertise at the critical point.

THE JOURNEY

Still, it was not easy. It is fair to say that the attitude of most employees was, "This too shall pass." ISO was regarded as a fad that required extra time from busy staff with no perceived benefit. Those of us in QI treated it as a political campaign and launched a broad initiative to reach every employee in every possible way. The motto was, "Constantly but politely in their faces." Our major efforts included these activities:

1. Dr. Brown attended every section meeting to confirm his support for ISO and to respond to questions (a few) and challenges (many). QI or our consultant occasionally provided follow-up if indicated.

2. The two QI employees met with all employees in their workspaces, one-on-one, to ask about their understanding of ISO, correct misconceptions, and offer assistance. This was a huge time commitment and was done only once, late in the preparation process.

3. We held brown-bag lunchtime meetings with no fixed agenda to answer questions. Some were useful and productive and some were not, but they were always available as a resource.

4. The director of QI wrote a one-paragraph e-mail message to all employees once a week on some aspect of ISO. These messages were aggregated into a single document that was available to everyone on the network.

5. QI wrote the quality manual with advice from our consultant. In retrospect, we believe that this was considerably over-written and too long, but it may have been necessary at that point in time. We set aside the first 30 minutes of the senior management meeting every week to review this manual, word by word. In addition to acquiring the requisite approval, these sessions served to acquaint every manager with every word in the manual in painful detail, together with the ISO standards behind them. The educational aspect of this approval process should not be minimized.

6. Auditing was virtually a continuous process. We did internal audits of each of our 30 key processes non-stop. Initially, these were done by our consultant with a new internal auditor in tow. We also did comprehensive, system-wide audits at three-month intervals during the last nine months. Initially these were done by our consultant, then by an independent auditor prior to our registration audit. These were useful in highlighting problem areas and confirming the urgency of corrective actions prior to our registration audit. They also confirmed the seriousness of the effort and the inevitability of the registration audit. When an auditor asked about the quality policy, no one was willing to respond, "I don't know, and I don't care." Similarly, no one wanted to be the section that caused the registration audit to fail.

7. Management review was ongoing. In the last quarter we did this almost every week, dedicating two to three hours of senior management time to review the results of the most recent internal audits or the practice external audits. These sessions kept senior management apprised of our status and identified problem areas under particular managers.

8. QI members made themselves available for consultations both spontaneous and scheduled. There were many phone calls: "Can you come over and help us with this? Now?" We did whatever we could to make this happen.

SUCCESS

The registration audit was almost anti-climactic. We were ready. We had been ready. There is a saying that "Smart people who work hard don't fail." While this may not be true in a competitive system where there must be a loser, it does apply to ISO, where everybody wins. We celebrated our success, including a photo-op with the under secretary for management. We wrote an article for the State Department magazine, and we moved on.

Our manual requires us to do a management review "at least once a year." By custom, we do them quarterly. Our goal is to achieve a status where appropriate metrics are used in the management of every section and shared with those employees regularly. We're not there yet. Some sections are still not measuring meaningful aspects of their processes. There is a tendency to count *how many* or *how much* without making an assessment of *how well*. Some sections regard reporting for management review as an exception, as an episodic requirement. Measurements are not made between reviews and not used in the management of their processes.

But there are also some successes. We have successfully combined several processes into a single "hiring process." Owners of parts of this process meet regularly to look at statistics and develop plans for improvement. At a recent meeting, someone asked why QI sought letters of reference for new applicants. "There is no HR requirement for these, and they are not useful in other parts of the hiring process." We stopped requesting these and deleted the peer reference form immediately. This change eliminated delays of up to a month in the hiring of some individuals. We're currently working on an on-line application process that would eliminate delays in obtaining the various forms required for a new application.

In some cases, improvements came as a result of measuring—no one knew how bad it was until they looked. The classic example is renewing a DEA application (a QI function). Initially, this could take up to 90 days and involved mail exchanges with overseas embassies. We took advantage of the DEA's interest in improving their process, and now the process takes only a few minutes, without any paper going anywhere.

Our second triennial audit took place without any special preparation. The focus of the auditors this time was to ensure that we had a management system in place and that we were using it. Although we still have one or two areas where participation is not perfect, ISO has become part of our culture. It is now accepted practice.

Most of the managers in MED are foreign service (FS) officers, so they rotate to a new assignment every three years. This means that almost every section in Washington gets a new chief every three years. ISO has played an important role in facilitating this transition by presenting the new manager with a written established procedure. "This is how we do things here, and we have data on how it is going." Procedures can be changed, but there is no need to re-invent a wheel that has been rolling for three years with acceptable results.

THE FUTURE

As managers rotate from Washington to assignments overseas, the ISO knowledge and experience go with them. This should facilitate our expansion of this system to the rest of the world in the near future.

A negative of this rotation scheme is that we lose a few of our internal auditors each time. We have tried to recruit internal auditors from a cross section of employees—from front line workers to managers—and to include both civil service and foreign service employees. To preserve this pattern, replacements are chosen carefully. There are three requirements for internal auditors:

1. **A willingness to serve.** Actually, we prefer enthusiasm.

2. **Permission of the supervisor.** This is formally done by both the employee and the management representative. Part of the agreement with the supervisor is to willingly allocate sufficient time for performance of up to four audits a year.

3. **Training.** Each internal auditor must have training by our outside consultant, generally in a Lead Auditor course.

The picture in MED is quite different now, as our QMS has matured. There are still a few reluctant participants, but they are mostly silent. The burden for the QI section has shifted from education and convincing employees to participate to helping various process owners with the selection of metrics and the collection, analysis, and presentation of data.

We still struggle with "meaningful metrics" and their use to improve processes. A frequent comment at management review is, "So what?" Process owners tend to present enumerative data—how many or how much, rather than evaluative data—how well. Both may be appropriate, and sometimes they are linked.

For example, two years ago, our clearance section showed that as they moved into their busy season, they reached a point where performance began to decline. It was taking longer to review the medical files and clear employees to serve overseas. The message at management review was obvious: If the time to issue a clearance is too long, you need to throw some more people into the production line.

We also struggle with getting sections to use metrics in the everyday running of their process. For many, data are analyzed and presented just before the quarterly management review meetings. This is one of the reasons we have management review quarterly instead of once a year.

When we reach a point where data are commonly used every day, we can move to annual management review meetings.

MOVING IT OVERSEAS

The longer-range challenge is moving this QMS to the overseas environment, but it's not as daunting as it might seem. For one thing, we have been seeding overseas health units with ISO-trained providers. Second, the overseas health unit is a fairly simple operation compared with Washington. A few of them have labs, but otherwise they are single-provider family practice clinics taking care of basically health people.

The real challenge for these locations is auditing. Some are thousands of miles from anyplace, and the plane only flies on Thursdays. We do have excellent electronic communication links, and it may be possible to do virtual audits from a distance.

SUMMARY

Our journey began with the realization that we had multiple little problems that resulted from not having a management system. There was no crisis—no single event—but once the decision was made, we had commitment. The day before our first registration audit, we surveyed all employees for their opinion of the program. The consensus opinion was that ISO was a good thing. Documents are easier to find now, and "stuff" happens faster.

There was no magic bullet. Inducing change in a bureaucracy requires consistent and credible effort. You have to do everything.

10

Experience with ISO 9001 in Healthcare Organizations

When ISO 9001 was introduced in 1987, it was clearly directed toward manufacturing; today it remains more common in industry than in healthcare. Corbett et al. demonstrated financial benefit for U.S. businesses that adopted ISO 9000,[1] but questioned whether the value was provided by the standard itself or by the internal and external auditing required. The real value of ISO 9000 began to gain hold after it was revised in year 2000 and renamed ISO 9001:2000. The standard, which subsequently underwent other minor cosmetic changes, is currently named ISO 9001:2008. The 2000 revision changed the target audience by catering to the needs of the service sector with enhanced concepts of customer satisfaction and continual improvement. This resulted in a standard that could be truly applicable to service organizations, including healthcare. In a 2010 study of 89 hospitals in six European countries, Shaw et al. reported significant differences in safety, management, and quality of clinical care at institutions that were either accredited locally or ISO 9001 registered compared to institutions that had neither.[2]

ACCREDITATION STANDARDS

In the United States there is a requirement for certification or accreditation of hospitals and other healthcare environments, primarily as a requirement for payment. There is no requirement for a management system, and this is an important distinction. The *Conditions of Participation* (CoP) from the Centers for Medicare and Medicaid Services (CMS) present accreditation standards but do not specify any management system, such as ISO 9001, as a tool for meeting the standards. Similarly, other accrediting organizations, such as The Joint Commission (TJC), require the meeting of standards but do not require a management system. Only DNV Healthcare, one of the largest certification bodies in the world, both sets standards (National Integrated Accreditation for

Healthcare Organizations, NIAHO) and requires a specific management system (ISO 9001). In a paper comparing accreditation systems, Vallejo et al. conclude that, "This new approach may strengthen the link between external oversight and the development of safe, effective, and efficient patient care processes."[3] Without a management system behind the standards compliance process, there is no consistent mechanism for reporting and dealing with problems. With a system such as ISO 9001, the compliance process is built into the way the company is run.

REHABILITATION FACILITIES

The State of Indiana accepts ISO registration as an alternative to accreditation by the Commission on Accreditation of Rehabilitation Facilities (CARF). This decision came after the documentation of benefits of ISO registration by several organizations providing services to handicapped citizens in Indiana. This began as a trial project, with the state sponsoring training for some rehabilitation facilities. The facilities that adopted ISO were motivated primarily by business reasons. They wanted contracts with businesses to employ their clients in light production work, and ISO registration earned respect from potential employers who were themselves registered. In some cases, the employers (automakers) required all suppliers to be ISO registered, so registration was required to bid on the job. When asked about benefits of ISO, many mentioned reduced costs of operation. These organizations are heavily dependent on local government subsidies and are typically poorly funded, so any improvement in efficiency means more services can be provided.

Occasionally, these organizations administer medications to clients under their care, and one CEO reported that medication errors virtually ceased with the introduction of a consistent medication administration procedure with ISO. This benefit could, of course, have been done without ISO, but it wasn't. The ISO standards provided the impetus to mandate explicit procedures for key processes, ensuring that everyone was doing it the same way—the right way.

Other than this example in Indiana, ISO registration per se is not accepted as a substitute for accreditation. They are, in fact, somewhat different concepts. ISO 9001 is a quality management system (QMS), a way of running the enterprise every day. An accreditation survey looks at the results of that QMS at periodic intervals. It is possible to do both. One of the rehabilitation facilities plans to incorporate the CARF standards into its QMS, so compliance with the CARF standards will be examined every quarter at management review.

HOSPITALS

For hospitals and most other healthcare institutions, accreditation by a third party has been a requirement for payment and is thus a cost of doing business. The Joint Commission captured most of this business because there were few alternatives. The essential requirement was to meet the *Conditions of Participation* defined by CMS, and these were included within the TJC standards for accreditation. Since the CoP were not included within ISO 9001, there was no perceived need to be scrutinized by yet another outside auditor. ISO certification of hospitals outside the United States is more common, because the lack of a requirement for accreditation render the external scrutiny provided with the ISO 9001 registration more valuable. The results vary with country and choice of registrar. DNV has issued more than 1200 certificates for healthcare-related organizations (hospitals, clinics, diagnostic centers, and the like) throughout the world outside of the United States. However, registration to ISO is less common in the United States.

CURRENT ENVIRONMENT

Healthcare has traditionally had a somewhat myopic viewpoint that denied the relevance of concepts outside the healthcare industry itself. However, this may be changing. When the Institute of Medicine (IOM) published *To Err is Human* in 2000, showing the extent of medical errors in hospitals, one of the ways hospitals found to seek remedies was to look outside of the hospital sector for improvement tools.[4] In 2005, in conjunction with the National Academy of Engineering, the IOM published *Building a Better Delivery System,* which advocated the use of quality improvement tools from industry.[5]

On 29 September 2008, the U.S. Government's Centers for Medicare and Medicaid Services (CMS) approved DNV Healthcare as an accreditation organization for hospitals—the first such approval in 40 years—enabling DNV to compete in a market long dominated by one accreditation organization, TJC. DNV accreditation is based on its NIAHO standards, an acronym for National Integrated Accreditation for Healthcare Organizations, which integrates the CMS *Conditions of Participation* with the quality management system principles from the international quality management system standard, ISO 9001:2008.

The DNV process requires accredited hospitals to become eligible for ISO registration within three years of their initial accreditation. Since DNV only began to accredit hospitals in 2008, it is now seeing the first group of hospitals come up for their triennial registration audit, which includes ISO 9001 eligibility.

ADVANTAGES OF USING ISO 9001:2008

The overall experience with the DNV accreditation process in hospitals has been positive, and employees have embraced the NIAHO and ISO standards as less onerous than other accreditation options. One executive told me, "The document control standard was an 'aha' experience for many employees, and that alone sold the concept."

One surprising benefit cited by management was that the required metrics and management review gave them a better picture of what was going on in their institution. You might think that senior management would always know what's going on, but there's nothing like having a chart front and center on the table. The management review standard within ISO 9001 requires senior management to review data on processes and outcomes from key processes in their organization at defined intervals.

Another comment from hospitals—and seconded by DNV—is that hospitals typically have 80% to 90% of the required mechanisms in place for DNV accreditation because of their prior history with TJC accreditation. In one large Texas hospital, employees were told specifically not to do any preparation for their first DNV / NIAHO survey. Their experience with a recent TJC survey enabled them to satisfy the NIAHO standards without additional effort. Hospitals have a culture of compliance with external standards, so switching from TJC to ISO or NIAHO does not represent a paradigm shift.

In some non-hospital settings, this tradition is not well established; any management system must provide definite value to be accepted.

The health units for all ships on the Cunard line are registered to ISO. One medical officer on the Queen Mary 2 said this allows him to serve on any ship in the fleet and know that the procedures and forms are exactly the same as his last ship. This consistency feature was also a factor in the selection by the State Department for its global system of health units where providers move every three years to a new location (see Chapter 9).

There is no central registry of ISO organizations, so it's not possible to know how many there are in any single industry. From conversations with registrars and consultants, however, it seems safe to say there are more in healthcare this year than last. In conversations with registered healthcare organizations, the most common benefit cited is "value." Managers feel they derive more value from an ISO audit than from audits by more traditional accreditation organizations. Another value frequently mentioned is internal audits. These give management a good picture of what is going on within the organization and also serve to acquaint employees from one area with what another section is doing.

Other advantages to ISO cited by organizations include:

1. There is only one management system in the institution, rather than one system for conducting business and another one for accreditation. This avoids waste from duplication of efforts.

2. The requirement for continual improvement means that the status quo is never good enough. Staff members are compelled to seek ways to improve operations and outcomes.

3. Internal audits have been mentioned before. Employees like doing these audits, and the required training teaches them about the management system.

4. Document control is one of the required procedures and frequently one of the more difficult to institute. Despite this, employees recognize the value of having needed documents readily available and generally embrace the concept.

5. Healthcare workers recognize patients as targets for their services. The ISO system brings other customers into view and broadens the concept of customer focus.

Every hospital we talked with reported no difficulty meeting the NIAHO standards in view of their TJC experience. Both standards incorporate the CoP as a basis. Most seem to have embraced the principles of ISO, but it remains to be seen if this will become a management system revolution in the healthcare industry. Many of the principles of ISO are included within the NIAHO standards, but some of the management system structure is new to the healthcare world.

References

1. C. J. Corbett, M. J. Montes-Sancho, and D. A. Kirsch, "The Financial Impact of ISO 9000 Certification in the US: An Empirical Analysis," *Management Science* 51: 1046–1059, July 2005.

2. C. Shaw, O. Groene, N. Mora, and R. Sunol, "Accreditation and ISO certification: do they explain differences in quality management in European Hospitals?" *International Journal for Quality in Health Care* 22: 445–451, October 2010.

3. B. C. Valleo, L. A. Flies, and D. J. Fine, "A Comparison of Hospital Accreditation Programs," *Journal of Clinical Engineering* 36: 32–38, Jan/Mar 2011.

4. L. T. Kohn, J. M. Corrigan, and M. S. Donaldson (eds.) *To Err is Human: Building a Safer Health System.* Institute of Medicine: National Academies Press, 2000.

5. P. P. Reid, W. D. Compton, J. H. Grossman, and G. Fanjiang (eds.) *Building a Better Delivery System: A New Engineering/Health Care Partnership.* National Academy of Engineering and Institute of Medicine: National Academies Press, 2005.

11

Utilization of ISO 9001 Concepts in the Community Setting: HIEs, PSOs, and ACOs

During the two and a half years that Physicians' Clinic of Iowa worked to establish its ISO 9001 QMS, a number of different ideas were generated that centered on the use of ISO 9001 principles in the community setting. This chapter describes some of the projects that were completed as well as potential applications in other areas of the community.

COMMUNITY ANTICOAGULATION THERAPY (CAT) CLINIC AND THE CEDAR RAPIDS HEALTHCARE ALLIANCE

In 2005, Physicians' Clinic of Iowa, in partnership with Kirkwood Community College in Cedar Rapids, was awarded a two-year grant entitled, *Improving Warfarin Management in Competitive Healthcare Using ISO 9001 Principles* (RFA–HS-05-012) by the Agency for Healthcare Research and Quality (AHRQ). The goal of this project was to create a community model of care delivery and patient safety using ISO 9001 principles as a framework of cooperation. The unique feature of the grant project was the utilization of ISO 9001 quality management system principles and concepts of Lean and Six Sigma (Lean-Six Sigma) to design the system of care that is currently being utilized in managing more than 400 patients of the anticoagulation clinic. Completing the grant employed ISO principles such as auditing and a controlled document system as well as Lean-Six Sigma principles including value stream mapping and Gage R and R to study workflow and variability. The project created a model of patient care and cooperation that addresses the issues of developing care delivery systems within a competitive environment. Furthermore, this model could likely be implemented in other communities. Specific tools that were developed include training materials on quality concepts related to ISO 9001, anticoagulation care guidelines, techniques for simplifying and controlling documents across multiple institutions and sites of care, and guidelines for utilizing auditing and corrective and preventive action plans to monitor clinical outcomes. A nonprofit entity, the Cedar Rapids Healthcare Alliance (CRHA), was initially established to oversee the anticoagulation clinic; it also provides the community infrastructure to support future projects and other healthcare initiatives. The CRHA has conducted quarterly community leadership forums since 2005 dealing with topics ranging from childhood obesity and employer wellness programs to data reporting, healthcare reform, and the new Cedar Rapids Medical District.

Figure 11.1 is a Community Anticoagulation Therapy (CAT) Clinic document that provides an overview of the services provided by the clinic. The ISO 9001-controlled document format includes a clear title and statement of purpose; the main body of the document describes the services. Appropriate records associated with the document are listed and a revision history is provided to ensure that the document used is current.

Document Title	Number	Rev.
Overview of CAT Clinic Services	3502CATC	1.0

Purpose (outline the intent or objective of the document)

To provide an overview of services of the CAT Clinic.

Definitions and Acronyms (provide clear understanding for words and abbreviations that may be ambiguous)

CAT Clinic – Community Anticoagulation Therapy Clinic

Procedure/Flowchart (describe the steps in which work objectives are achieved; include statements, to the extent necessary, that explain the *why, what, when, where, who,* and *how*)

1. The CAT Clinic will provide the following services to its patients:
   - Assess the patient for risk of complications related to anticoagulation therapy.
   - Manage the patient's anticoagulation therapy with the referring physician via a signed guideline approved by the CAT Clinic medical director.
   - Provide education about anticoagulation therapy to the patient and significant others.
   - Maximize the benefits of anticoagulation therapy by collecting data to show percent of patients in range, missed labs per patient, patient and provider satisfaction with the program, and complications requiring hospitalization.

2. The RN providing care to patients enrolled in the CAT Clinic will have the following qualifications:
   - A valid Registered Nursing License in the state of Iowa.
   - Completion of the Anticoagulation Therapy Management Certificate program within six months of hire.
   - Excellent interpersonal and customer service skills.

Figure 11.1 Example of an anticoagulation clinic document in ISO format. *(Continued)*

(Continued)

Procedure/Flowchart (describe the steps in which work objectives are achieved; include statements, to the extent necessary, that explain the *why, what, when, where, who,* and *how*)

Physicians referring patients to the CAT Clinic will have the following responsibilities:

- Complete a CAT Clinic Referral Standing Order form for each patient referred to the clinic.
- Inform the patient about referral and enrollment in the CAT Clinic.
- Respond to inquiries from the CAT Clinic nurse in a timely manner.
- Continue to address clinical concerns outside of anticoagulation therapy.
- Contact the CAT Clinic nurse with changes that may affect anticoagulation therapy (change in medications, knowledge of surgical procedure, and so on).
- Collaborate with the CAT Clinic nurse regarding non-compliant patients and patients who may be discharged for non-compliance or completion of therapy.
- Contact the CAT Clinic if patient expires or the physician withdraws the patient from his/her service.
- In the absence of the referring physician, there shall be a physician on call and available for consultation.

3. The CAT Clinic nurse will have the following responsibilities:
   - Review all new referrals and orders and contact the referring physician with any questions or concerns.
   - Educate the referring physician's office staff about CAT Clinic services.
   - Inform the referring physicians that standing orders for Coumadin®/warfarin management and refills are good for one year.
   - Provide a new referral form to the referring physician annually for each patient enrolled in the CAT Clinic.
   - Follow the established anticoagulation guideline. Notify the physician when International Normalized Ratio (INR) values are out-of-range, or if the patient reports problems that cannot be handled by the CAT Clinic nurse.
   - Communicate in writing or via the telephone (if the INR is out of range) with the referring physician each time an INR result is received.
   - Refer patients for a physician visit when necessary and consult with the referring physician for urgent situations.

4. The CAT Clinic Medical Director will have the following responsibilities.
   - Approve all CAT Clinic policies, procedures, and guidelines before implementation.
   - Approve revisions to CAT Clinic policies, procedures, and guidelines.
   - Serve as a contact for the CAT Clinic nurse for questions and concerns.

5. Discontinuation of responsibilities of the CAT Clinic medical director and CAT Clinic nurse:
   - The medical director or CAT Clinic nurse are not responsible for a patient's anticoagulation management if the warfarin is being adjusted, held, or monitored by any provider that is not the referring physician.

Figure 11.1 Example of an anticoagulation clinic document in ISO format.

(Continued)

Records: (Results or evidence of work performed.)	
Referral Standing Order	6002CATC
Introduction Letter	4501CATC
Warfarin Guideline for INR Target Range of 2-3	6511CATC
Warfarin Guideline for INR Range of 2.5-3.5	6512CATC
Physician Communication Record	6004CATC

REVISION HISTORY			
Revision	Description of Change	Approval	Date
0	Initial document	J. Levett, MD	12-16-05
1	Changed protocol to guideline	J. Levett, MD	2-24-06

Figure 11.1 Example of an anticoagulation clinic document in ISO format.

The use of ISO 9001 principles in the community setting may be expanded to include other types of projects. This is of particular importance in the present era of healthcare reform with the significant budget challenges facing the healthcare sector.

A LEAN PROJECT FOR THE COMMUNITY

In March 2008, the Cedar Rapids Healthcare Alliance was awarded a grant by the Iowa Foundation for Medical Care to conduct a Lean project focused on common healthcare processes. The CRHA, working with two of its support partners, the Cedar Rapids Physician Hospital Organization (PHO) and the Iowa Quality Center, began identifying administrative concerns within local medical offices. The Cedar Rapids PHO conducted a survey of twelve office managers to identify tasks or issues that were burdensome to provider offices. This survey document was e-mailed to 120 offices; 43 were returned for a 36% return rate. The survey found a number of issues that were of concern to the office managers, and six of these were addressed in the course of the 12-month study.

Throughout 2008–2009, six Lean teams were formed in Cedar Rapids using the Iowa Quality Center personnel for facilitation and Lean expertise. Area administrators gathered to streamline processes, identify waste, share best practices, and develop policies to reduce cost and administrative burden to medical practices. Participating entities included the two local hospitals, laboratories, primary care and specialty physician offices, and an outpatient imaging center.

The teams focused on the following topics:

- Team 1 – Improving the registration process for patients and medical practices
- Team 2 – Improving the electronic transfer of information between hospitals and medical practices
- Team 3 – Developing a community standard for appropriately documenting consultations and referrals
- Team 4 – Streamlining and improving collection processes
- Team 5 – Developing a FTC-compliant Red Flag Rules policy
- Team 6 – Sharing best practices in medical human resource management

The provider entities participated in a series of Lean *kaizen* events to focus on one process at a time in order to map the process for each entity, determine common issues and problems, and identify best practices (Figures 11.2 and 11.3). The primary goal was to streamline administrative processes that impact patient care, and eventually to create more standard work for these organizations. The Lean methodology used in the project is consistent with conventional Lean techniques. The first team addressed the issue of registration and established the working examples for the other teams.

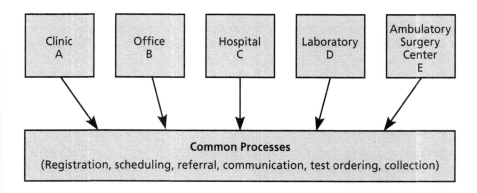

Figure 11.2 Common healthcare processes.

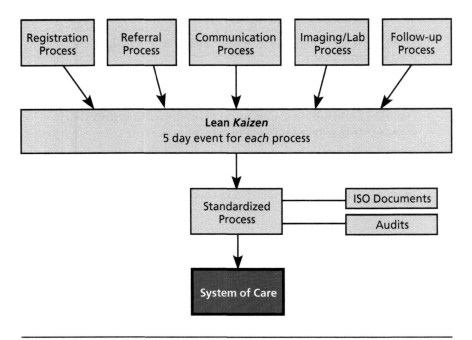

Figure 11.3 Developing a community "system of care."

Lean Team 1: Registration

Lean Team 1 developed the model that subsequent teams followed. This initial team included providers from a wide spectrum of area healthcare facilities, ranging from primary care physician clinics to specialty medical services. In this team, 15 clinic, office, and hospital representatives came together to study the delivery and efficiency of their registration processes. This type of problem involved, on average, about 10% of the patients in the clinic registration process; some clinics experienced up to 20% because patients were not available to verify the information during the registration process. The team began with four hours of Lean training and a high-level overview of each clinic's registration process. There were six subsequent four-hour meetings during which participants studied the current situation through collection of data and observations regarding these registration processes.

Data, measures, and work processes included:

- Value stream maps: an average of six were completed for the registration process.
- Steps: an average of six high-level steps were identified
- Time to register: an average time of seven minutes was noted for several clinics.

- Time when no registration information is available: an average 20-minute wait was identified.
- Time to register with changes: an average 10-minute time for rework and defect correction was identified.
- Implementation of best practice: time to register was noted to be 3 to 5 minutes.
- Implementation of best practices: estimated to save between 5 and 10 minutes depending on the practice and culture of the clinic.
- Time to rework errors in registration data, which was usually provided by another entity or the patient: found to be 20 to 60 minutes per case.

The group quickly noted that their processes shared common features, even though they practiced at different clinics. The team then established a clear and common goal: accurate and timely collection of demographic data (name, mailing address, phone, and insurance information). Focusing on their common goal, the team brainstormed, researched, and piloted several ideas for best practices that all clinics on the team could potentially use to supplement their individual processes. The researchers and pilot leaders reported to the entire team, which then discussed and reviewed the opportunities for improvement.

Best practices identified include:

- Pre-verification before the visit
- Verification process / electronic eligibility
- Post-verification if not available at visit
- Date stamp copy of insurance cards
- Switch scripting with patient at the check-in process
- Scripting with referring offices and passing information among clinics
- Send reports with errors to those entities
- Establish database of patient information and develop a swipe card process

Key points learned from Lean Team 1:

- Streamline communication and transfer of information
- Develop a swipe card process
- Implement consistent scripting and processes by registration staff
- More education and training needed

Cost savings identified by Lean Team 1 included:

- Saved: Average 140 min/clinic/week in registration time
  - Dollars: (@ $20/hour - $46 per clinic) ~$370/week saved for 8 clinics
- Saved: Average 17.5 hours/week/clinic with other improvements
  - Dollars: (@ $20/hour) ~$350/clinic/week
- Total cost savings for the community resulting from the work of the six Lean teams is estimated at more than $200,000 annually

Two aspects of this project are worth noting. First, although this was a Lean project, the ideas were developed using the familiar process approach described in this book. In addition, the work of standardizing processes and procedures throughout the community is ongoing and should be supported by an ISO document system which, in the future, may include an audit function.

HEALTH INFORMATION EXCHANGES: THE FUTURE OF HEALTHCARE IT

An important aspect of the Patient Protection and Affordable Care Act (PPACA) of 2010 is the health IT component of the bill, the HITECH Act, which appropriates $19.2 billion dollars to encourage the adoption of electronic health records (EHR). The payments are structured as incentives and are triggered when a provider or hospital demonstrates it has become a "meaningful EHR user." Depending upon the individual physician's payor mix, qualified physicians will receive incentive payments through additional reimbursements via either Medicare or Medicaid beginning in 2011. These qualified users can earn $44,000 under the Medicare plan and $64,000 under the Medicaid plan over five years. Those joining the program early will gain the most benefit, since about 70% of the payments are made in the first two years. Physicians who do not adopt an EHR by 2015 will be penalized by decreases in Medicare reimbursements rates.

Using an EHR is a necessary first step in developing health IT systems. The goal is to link EHRs and IT systems among provider groups within a community, then statewide, and eventually on a national basis. These local systems are termed health information exchanges (HIEs). As with other types of community projects, developing HIEs could be facilitated using an ISO QMS platform with a common and controlled document system, corrective and preventive action plans, and auditing to ensure compliance.

PATIENT SAFETY ORGANIZATIONS (PSOS)

The Patient Safety and Quality Improvement Act of 2005 (Patient Safety Act) authorized the creation of PSOs as voluntary entities with a mission to improve both quality and patient safety through the collection and analysis of data on patient events. Organizations that are eligible to become PSOs include: public or private entities, for-profit or not-for-profit entities, provider entities such as hospital chains, and other entities that establish special components to serve as PSOs. PSOs collect patient safety data and maintain confidentiality, thereby creating a secure environment where clinicians and healthcare organizations can collect, aggregate, analyze, and discuss quality and patient safety data. In this way, providers will improve quality and reduce the risks and hazards associated with patient care. There are currently 80 PSOs in 30 states and the District of Columbia listed by AHRQ on its website www.pso.ahrq.gov.

PSOs create a patient safety work product that is protected information, and carry out patient safety activities as described by AHRQ. Eight patient safety activities are carried out by, or on behalf of, a PSO or a healthcare provider:

- Efforts to improve patient safety and the quality of healthcare delivery
- The collection and analysis of patient safety work product (PSWP)
- The development and dissemination of information regarding patient safety, such as recommendations, protocols, and information regarding best practices
- The utilization of PSWP for the purposes of encouraging a culture of safety and providing feedback and assistance to effectively minimize patient risk
- The maintenance of procedures to preserve confidentiality with respect to PSWP
- The provision of appropriate security measures with respect to PSWP
- The utilization of qualified staff
- Activities related to the operation of a patient safety evaluation system and to the provision of feedback to participants in a patient safety evaluation system

Chapter 8 discussed the idea that a QMS could provide the foundation for a performance improvement system and assist an organization in developing a risk assessment program. The same concepts apply to setting up a PSO, including the use of operational definitions within the controlled document system, using the documents to clarify reporting relationships, and utilizing auditing to ensure that the reporting is being done according to defined procedures.

ISO 9001 AS A FRAMEWORK FOR ACCOUNTABLE CARE ORGANIZATIONS AND POPULATION HEALTH MANAGEMENT

The Patient Protection and Affordable Care Act of 2010 describes the concept of accountable care organizations (ACOs), which will be established to facilitate coordination and cooperation among providers in order to reduce costs and improve the quality of care for Medicare beneficiaries. An accountable care organization is "an organization of healthcare providers that agrees to be accountable for the quality, cost, and overall care of Medicare beneficiaries who are enrolled in the traditional fee-for-service program or who are assigned to it."[1] ACOs will initially cover Medicare patients under a fee-for-service payment system. It is anticipated, however, that many different types of ACOs will evolve and will include varying types of risk arrangements and potentially non fee-for-service payment structures. Another key aspect of their mission will be population health management and the inclusion of public health expertise and measures.

The first question has to do with what systems and frameworks will be utilized to support the development of ACOs. Current quality improvement systems used in healthcare organizations and businesses are not easily applied to population health management and changing complex adaptive systems. Care orientation will change as providers move from a production-oriented system of care (for example, standard treatments for acute illnesses, number of repeatable procedures per hour) to a less predictable and evolving system of health risks and behaviors that are constantly changing in response to multiple factors. In conventional healthcare delivery, technology is often the driver of changes observed in healthcare outcomes for acute, episodic care. Within population health management, behaviors—influenced by social networks, media, clinicians, and many other factors—become the predominant force affecting health status, future costs, and health outcomes.

This line of reasoning suggests that a quality management approach to ACOs and population health must operate within a new set of parameters. ACOs need a quality framework, not a recipe, for management of outcomes in a population. A quality management system approach can provide the organization with the necessary structure and control to achieve sustained success with complex systems. The following quality principles for population health management have been compared with the ISO 9001 principles (Table 11.1).

Table 11.1 Comparing ISO 9001 and population health management principles.

ISO 9001	Population Health Management
Leadership	Community-based leadership
Customer focus	Patient- and clinician-centered focus
Systems approach to management	Service integration across the continuum of health
Process approach	Changing complex adaptive systems
Fact-based decision making	Population-based risk management
Involvement of people	Social networks
Continuous improvement	Responsiveness to an evolving system through rapid-cycle improvement
Mutually beneficial supplier relationships	Stakeholder integration

Community-based Leadership

Comprehensive population health management requires collaborative leadership that can extend beyond a single organization and align multiple stakeholders throughout the community. Experience with the Cedar Rapids Healthcare Alliance would suggest that the key is to include all sectors of the community—business, government, education, public health, free clinics, and traditional providers such as hospitals, laboratories, physicians, and nurses.

Patient- and Clinician-centered Focus

The most important health relationship for most people is the relationship with a primary clinician(s). Population health programs are increasingly emphasizing the idea of extending these relationships to create virtual extensions of the clinical team, including health educators, health coaches, and other community-based resources in an aligned and organized approach.

Service Integration Across the Continuum of Health

The highest engagement rates by participants in population health management programs are achieved by programs that emphasize a high level of communication and referrals among services across the continuum. To achieve this integration, significant work in process re-engineering, workflow management, and communication systems is required on an ongoing basis at the level of the individual patients as well as that of the population.

Changing Complex Adaptive Systems

According to Plsek, the change process for complex adaptive systems in population health management is characterized by: (1) clarity of direction as well as measurable goals; (2) simple structures and constraints; (3) reinforcement of the desired direction by people–activities in the clinical, worksite, home, community and social network environments; (4) rapid-cycle improvement in response to continuous feedback; and (5) anticipation of and flexibility to respond to natural variation within a range.[2]

Population-based Risk Management

Achieving sustainable outcomes in population health management requires a focus on identifying, quantifying, and addressing underlying risk factors for the population at large. This requires a multiple-stakeholder approach to collaboration and public health expertise.

Social Networks

Unlike more traditional systems found in current medical care delivery, population health management processes are far more dependent upon personal relationships and influences from various social networks. Ignoring social networks and not formally incorporating them in the processes is shortsighted and can lead to unexplained deviations from the expected outcomes for a complex system.

Responsiveness to an Evolving System through Rapid-cycle Improvement

Population health management programs need continuous feedback on both an individual and population level and the flexibility to rapidly respond to new circumstances within the community and overall healthcare delivery system.

Stakeholder Integration

As stated above, population health management requires the coordination of multiple stakeholders (including the patient, family/friends, clinician, employer, health plan, and community) into an organized system with mutually beneficial relationships aligned around common and measureable goals.

Figure 11.4 is an example of a quality system model for population health management incorporating some of the concepts and principles described above (used with permission of Roberts Health Solutions).

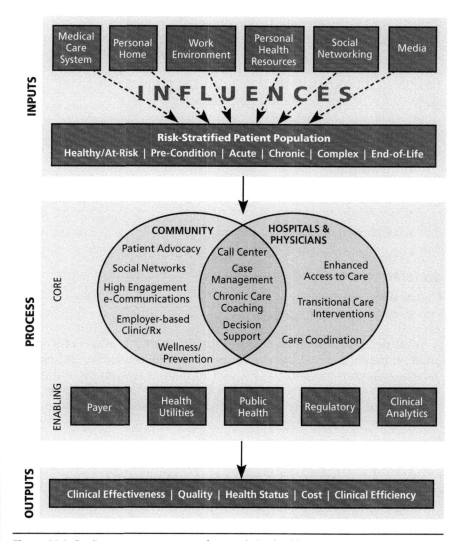

Figure 11.4 Quality management system for population health.

The population health quality system illustrated in Figure 11.4 was developed using the process approach described in Chapter 1. This system begins by identifying the diverse influences on the ACO population as inputs that influence the patient population and includes many factors. For purposes of analysis, the population is risk-stratified and adjusted to better understand the inherent risks for which the ACO is assuming responsibility. The ACO, set in the context of the community, is the driver of the various core processes. The core processes can reside in the ACO or the community, depending on the resources and needs of the local community. The enabling processes are supportive for both the ACO and the community. The outputs of the system are both process and outcome measures that are used to: (1) measure progress against a baseline; (2) benchmark with other ACOs; (3) establish goals; and (4) develop a scorecard for monitoring and reporting.

The key functions and processes of an ACO include the following:

- Chronic disease management
- Contracting
- Governance
- Guideline development, best practices
- IT, clinical information systems
- Payment structures
- Development and tracking of performance metrics
- Risk assessment
- Utilization and case management

Critical decisions made by an ACO involve multiple stakeholders from many different parts of the community. Clinical, economic, and political factors influence these decisions, and in many cases multiple inputs to the process must be considered. For this reason a systems approach is quite useful in designing an entity that will be sustainable and provide value as it evolves.

MOVING TOWARD A QUALITY SYSTEM AT THE COMMUNITY LEVEL

The experiences from the community projects described above have been of benefit to many local provider entities. They illustrate how to reduce variation, avoid rework, and standardize processes within the community. One of the current topics of discussion at quarterly CRHA meetings is potentially adopting the Institute for Healthcare Improvement's triple aim of delivering high quality care to the individual and managing the health of the population at a low cost. The idea of using ISO principles to develop a quality management system at the community level has also been discussed (Figure 11.5), continuing the work begun in 2005 with the AHRQ grant to establish a community anticoagulation clinic using ISO 9001 principles. Such a quality system could initially define customer requirements from all sectors of the community and the QMS infrastructure could be used to serve other functions such as those related to data collection, data exchange (HIE),

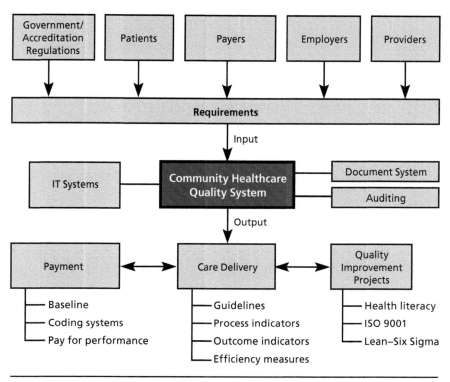

Figure 11.5 A community healthcare quality system.

data analysis, document control, and creation of interoperable systems linked via information technology and process/policy/procedure features. Standardization of community systems in this way would facilitate information sharing, knowledge transfer, and ongoing evaluation and quality improvement. The system outputs would include payment, care delivery, and quality improvement projects, among others. Appropriate goals, objectives, and measures could be developed, tracked, and audited within the context of the QMS described in this book. Thus the real value of using a quality system is that it not only outlines a framework to organize the factors influencing the business, organization, or process, but also provides practical tools to utilize in managing those factors, such as auditing, a document system, and management review.

References

1. www.cms.gov/OfficeofLegislation/Downloads/ AccountableCareOrganization.pdf

2. P. E. Plsek, *Creativity, Innovation and Quality.* (Milwaukee: Quality Press, 1997).

Index

Page numbers in *italics* refer to tables and figures.

A

accountable care organizations (ACO), xiii, 108, 111–112
accounts receivable, 78
accreditation standards, 93–94
ACO (accountable care organizations), 108, 111–112
adverse events, 50, 70
Agency for Healthcare Research and Quality (AHRQ), 43, 99–102, 112
AHRQ survey of patient safety, 43
American National Standards Institute (ANSI), 10, 11, 75
American Recovery and Reinvestment Act (2009), 72
American Society for Quality, 9
anticoagulation clinic, 99–102, *100*
auditing, 15, 35, 77, 83, 88
audits, *4, 7*
automotive industry, QMS and, xvii, 1, 9
Automotive Industry Action Group (AIAG), 9

B

balanced scorecard, *5, 7, 8,* 51, 67–69
Baldrige Award Healthcare Criteria, 51–52
Baldrige Criteria for Performance Excellence, 86
best practices, 105
Brown, Larry, 86, 87

budgets, culture and, 42–43
"Building a Better Delivery System" (National Academy of Engineering), 95
Business Operating Systems (BOS) for Health Care Organizations, 10

C

care delivery systems, 99
CARF (Commission on Accreditation of Rehabilitation Facilities), 94
Carlzon, Jan, 21
Cedar Rapids Healthcare Alliance (CRHA), 99–106
Cedar Rapids Physician Hospital Organization (PHO), 102–104
CEO responsibility, 42–43
change, factors driving, xxi
change, resistance to, 43–46
chief executive officer (CEO) responsibility, 42–43
clinical integration, 57, *59,* 59–62
clinical patient flow process, *29, 30, 83*
clinical quality measures, 73, 80–81
clinician-centered focus, 109
Clinton, Hillary, 44
Commission on Accreditation of Rehabilitation Facilities (CARF), 94
communication, 19, 37, 44, 45, 88–89
Community Anticoagulation Therapy (CAT) Clinic, 99–102, *100, 102*
community-based leadership, 109

HIPAA requirements, 77
hiring process, 89
HITECH Act, 106
"home training," 41
hospital-acquired conditions, 70
hospitals, ISO in, 95, 96

I

IFMC (Iowa Foundation for Medical
    Care), 81, 102–104
improvement, 65
*Improving Warfarin Management in
    Competitive Healthcare Using
    ISO 9001 Principles,* 99–102
inclusion, quality manual and, 16
Indiana rehabilitation facilities, 94
individual roles, 44
individual standards, 15–20
inputs and outputs, 3, *4*
Institute for Healthcare Improvement,
    112
Institute of Medicine (IOM)
    To Err is Human, 95
Internal Audit (clause 8.2.2), 32
internal auditing, 35, 64, 83, 88, 90
international implications of ISO,
    89–90
International Organization for
    Standardization (ISO)
    customer focus, 20–21
    foundation of, 9
    individual standards, 15–20
    original purpose, 9, 75
    overview, 11–12
    principles for healthcare, 12–15
    world implementation, 9
inventory as waste, 52, 53
Iowa Foundation for Medical Care
    (IFMC), 81, 102–104
Iowa Quality Center, 102–104
ISO certification for healthcare, xxi,
    10, 86, 97
ISO quality management systems.
    See quality management systems

ISO standards
    background and requirements,
        75–76
    and clinical integration, 60–61
    flexibility and brevity of, 11–12
    overview, 11
    quality management principles, 76
    universal applicability of, 12
    versatility of, 49
ISO terminology, 16
IWA-1 healthcare document, 9

J

The Joint Commission, 49, 86, 93

K

kaizen events, 79, 103, *104*
Kaplan, R., 8, 67–69
key processes, 3, *4, 5*
    identifying and mapping, 26–27
    managing, 4–5
    U.S. State Department, 88
Kirkwood Community College,
    99–102

L

Lead Auditors, 87
leadership commitment, 24–25
Lean, 2, 52–54, 79, 99–102
Lean community project, 102–104

M

Machiavelli on change, 43
Malcolm Baldrige National Quality
    Award, 1, 12, 51–52, 86
management responsibility (Section
    5), 18, 24–25
management review, *4, 7,* 64, 88, 89, 96
management review meetings, 77
mapping, process, 26, 57–59
meaningful metrics, 90
meaningful use, xiii, 60, 72–74, 106

U

U.S. State Department
  audits, 46
  business model, 85
  communication model, 87–88
  competence assessment, 51–52
  international implications of ISO,
    89–90, 91
  ISO evaluation process, 86
  ISO implementation costs, 87
  organizational culture, 44
  registration audit, 89
  root cause analysis, 50

V

value stream mapping, 79

W-X-Y-Z

waiting as waste, 52, 53
waste, seven types of, 52, 53–54
work flow, 26–30
work instructions, 32
workers' compensation claims, 80, *81*
wound infections, 82
written procedures, 34

Belong to the Quality Community!

Established in 1946, ASQ is a global community of quality experts in all fields and industries. ASQ is dedicated to the promotion and advancement of quality tools, principles, and practices in the workplace and in the community.

The Society also serves as an advocate for quality. Its members have informed and advised the U.S. Congress, government agencies, state legislatures, and other groups and individuals worldwide on quality-related topics.

Vision

By making quality a global priority, an organizational imperative, and a personal ethic, ASQ becomes the community of choice for everyone who seeks quality technology, concepts, or tools to improve themselves and their world.

ASQ is...

- More than 90,000 individuals and 700 companies in more than 100 countries

- The world's largest organization dedicated to promoting quality

- A community of professionals striving to bring quality to their work and their lives

- The administrator of the Malcolm Baldrige National Quality Award

- A supporter of quality in all sectors including manufacturing, service, healthcare, government, and education

- YOU

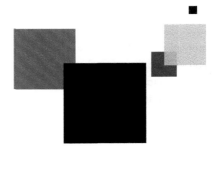

Visit www.asq.org for more information.

ASQ Membership

Research shows that people who join associations experience increased job satisfaction, earn more, and are generally happier.* ASQ membership can help you achieve this while providing the tools you need to be successful in your industry and to distinguish yourself from your competition. So why wouldn't you want to be a part of ASQ?

Networking

Have the opportunity to meet, communicate, and collaborate with your peers within the quality community through conferences and local ASQ section meetings, ASQ forums or divisions, ASQ Communities of Quality discussion boards, and more.

Professional Development

Access a wide variety of professional development tools such as books, training, and certifications at a discounted price. Also, ASQ certifications and the ASQ Career Center help enhance your quality knowledge and take your career to the next level.

Solutions

Find answers to all your quality problems, big and small, with ASQ's Knowledge Center, mentoring program, various e-newsletters, *Quality Progress* magazine, and industry-specific products.

Access to Information

Learn classic and current quality principles and theories in ASQ's Quality Information Center (QIC), *ASQ Weekly* e-newsletter, and product offerings.

Advocacy Programs

ASQ helps create a better community, government, and world through initiatives that include social responsibility, Washington advocacy, and Community Good Works.

Visit www.asq.org/membership for more information on ASQ membership.

*2008, The William E. Smith Institute for Association Research